FEEDING MY ARMY

To Bev – fellow army wife!

Hope you enjoy the book!

Best wishes,

Beca
X

First published in 2020 by Gomer Press,
Llandysul, Ceredigion SA44 4JL

ISBN 978-1-78562-329-5

A CIP record for this title is available from the British Library.

Text © Beca Lyne-Pirkis, 2020
Photographs © Aled Llywelyn 2020

Design: Rebecca Ingleby Davies

This book is published with the financial support of
The Books Council of Wales.

Printed and bound in Wales at
Gomer Press, Llandysul, Ceredigion
www.gomer.co.uk

FEEDING MY ARMY

Beca Lyne-Pirkis

Gomer

CONTENTS

INTRODUCTION

They say that an army marches on its stomach and as a proud army wife, I would agree wholeheartedly that food is central to military life. My husband, Matthew, who is currently a staff sergeant with the Royal Army Medical Corps, has an endless supply of stories which span his career from basic training to his most recent operational tour to Afghanistan, many of which revolve around food.

This book taps into that rich vein of army experience and also draws inspiration from the three remarkable women in my life who lived through the Second World War – my grandmothers, Nan and Mam-gu, along with Aunty 'Rene, who fell in love and married a wartime American sailor. They've all had a huge influence on me in the kitchen, and so many of the recipes I've included in this book - from rationing and food coupons; postings abroad; catering on the home front; feeding my own hungry little troops; cooking for one while Matt is overseas doing his day job; ration packs on rain-sodden mountainsides to a makeshift cookhouse in a warzone – have been inspired by them.

I hope these recipes will give you an insight into the nurturing power of food from the perspective of the military community, not only for those serving in the forces but for those who dutifully keep the home fires burning.

Times can be tough, but there are some amazing moments too, especially when your solider returns home after months away – despite the tendency to completely mess up a well-oiled routine that has worked like clockwork while they've been away.

I'm very proud of my husband, all his colleagues and all my family members who have served over the years, and I dedicate this book to them. I hope it contains something for everyone, be it cooking your own solo suppers, your family favourites and feeding your very own army.

CHAPTER 1

MAKE DO AND DIG FOR VICTORY

Nan and Aunty Irene were born between the two world wars. Mam-gu, my other grandmother, lived through both wars during an era filled with fear and difficult challenges. All three experienced life and rations very differently, with Mam-gu being able to feed her family from what they had on the farm, my great aunt marrying and emigrating to America and my nan living, working and falling in love during the Second World War. These three phenomenal women faced these challenges in their own special way. To them it was life and they took it all in their stride.

Their lives were tough, but the stories I heard from them and still get to hear from Nan are all happy memories filled with love and laughter. Rationing was strict and yet they managed to find ways around all the rules to cook delicious meals for their families and bake birthday and wedding cakes with the help of their communities. Some of the recipes are ones that should remain buried in history, but many have stood the test of time and are still cooked today. Some simple recipes which allowed the ingredients to sing were very popular.

They made use of leftovers during a time when waste was discouraged – a lesson that should still apply today.

BEER & CHEESE SODA BREAD

In 1935, a small brewery in Llanelli began producing its beer in cans. By using its family links in the tinplate industry and closely observing what the big brewers were doing across the pond in America, Felinfoel Brewery was the first to can beer in Wales, the UK and Europe. The brewery was the only one allowed to can and sell beer for the home market during the Second World War and additional batches were sent to the troops abroad, wherever they were based.

In honour of this feat of engineering and brewing, here's my favourite recipe for soda bread; a bread that both my grandmothers would make and bake if yeast wasn't available. However they didn't use beer or cheese in their loaves!

MAKES 1 LOAF

180g self-raising brown flour

160g spelt flour, plus extra for dusting

½ tsp salt

1 tsp bicarbonate of soda

150g extra mature or vintage Cheddar cheese, cut into 1cm cubes

280ml beer

prep: 15-20 minutes, cook: 30 minutes

Preheat the oven to 200°C fan/220°C/gas mark 7, and line a baking tray with greaseproof paper, dusted with flour.

Place the flours, salt, bicarbonate of soda and cheese cubes in a mixing bowl and stir to combine. Make a well in the middle, add the beer and bring the dough into a ball using a dough scraper or a spatula.

Tip the dough out onto a flour-dusted surface. Roughly shape it into a ball and place on the prepared baking tray – it will be sticky, so don't handle it too much.

Use a sharp knife to make a cross in the dough. Bake in the oven for 30 minutes and leave to cool slightly before slicing.

AUNTY 'RENE'S SLOPPY JOES & MEATLOAF

Here are two great American classics: Sloppy Joes and meatloaf. Enjoy both with mashed potatoes and some green vegetables or in a soft bread roll.

While looking through Aunty 'Rene's recipe box, I came across five different recipes for meatloaf which made me think that it was a family favourite, however my cousin Patty told me that she never had meatloaf at home. Maybe it was one of those recipes that Aunty 'Rene wanted to have in her armoury just in case.

I've had the Sloppy Joe in a sandwich and although it was tasty it was very messy to eat.

SERVES 4-6

40g chopped onion

45g green pepper, diced

2 tbsp oil

450g/1lb hamburger/steak mince

½ tbsp lemon juice

½ tsp chilli powder

tin of tomato soup

salt and pepper to taste

1 tsp Worcestershire sauce

SLOPPY JOES

prep: 10 minutes, cook: 40 minutes

Heat the oil over a medium-high heat and brown the meat. Add the chopped and diced onion and pepper and cook for a few minutes. Add the remaining ingredients and simmer for 30 minutes. Taste to check the seasoning halfway and add salt, pepper and Worcestershire sauce as needed. Serve in a soft bread roll (see the bread roll recipe page 124) or with creamy mash and vegetables.

SERVES 10

60g of breadcrumbs

250ml milk

675g/1½lbs minced beef

2 beaten eggs

40g chopped onion

1 tsp salt

½ tsp pepper

½ tsp dried sage

For the sauce

3 tbsp brown sugar

2 tsp Dijon mustard

4 tbsp ketchup

MEATLOAF

prep: 15 minutes, cook: up to 1 hour

Preheat the oven to 170°C fan/190°C/gas mark 5.

Soak the breadcrumbs in the milk and add the remaining meatloaf ingredients. Mix well and place in a loaf tin/s ready for baking. The mixture makes one large 2lb loaf or two small 1lb loaves.

Make the sauce from the sugar mustard and ketchup and coat the loaf/loaves. Bake for 45 minutes – 1 hour for the larger loaf, and about 35-45 minutes for the smaller loaves.

Serve the meatloaf hot in a sandwich with more mustard and some gherkins, or with creamy mash and greens.

It's a staple dish served in the American forces' chow halls and a firm favourite amongst the troops.

AUNTY 'RENE'S APPLE CAKE

My aunty 'Rene was a phenomenal woman. When she was nineteen, during the Second World War, she married a dashing young American sailor, waved goodbye to her family in Splott, Cardiff and boarded a US Navy transport with 109 other foreign wives to be reunited with her sweetheart in America. Uncle John and Aunty Irene eventually settled in St Louis, Missouri where they had five children.

I have very fond memories of visiting the family when I was a little eight-year-old girl. I could, more often than not, be found in the kitchen attached to Aunty 'Rene's hip, watching her every move, helping when I could and absorbing everything, tasting and making mental notes of all that she made in that kitchen.

The sadness that came over me when I was told that Aunty 'Rene had passed away is something that has stayed with me. I wished I had lived closer and had been able to spend more time with her. However, the time I did get to spend with her was very special and has had a great impact on me personally and professionally.

Aunty 'Rene's food was always delicious but simple. Here's a warming apple cake that can be enjoyed as a dessert or with a cup of tea mid-morning. It's a celebration cake in honour of those young brides who set sail to meet up with their new husbands in a strange land which was to become their new home.

SERVES 12

340g of light-brown sugar

110g butter, unsalted

2 eggs

280g plain flour

2 tsp bicarbonate of soda

1 tsp salt

1 tsp cinnamon

1 tsp nutmeg

1 tsp allspice

580g diced eating apples, half peeled and half with skin on

75g walnuts

110g sultanas

prep: 20 minutes, cook: 1 hour

Preheat oven to 150°C fan/170°C/gas mark 3 and grease and line a 9-inch x 13-inch / 23cm x 32cm tin and set to one side.

Cream the sugar and butter until light and add the eggs one at a time, mixing well between the addition of each one. Sieve the dry ingredients into the bowl and mix thoroughly (mixture will feel stiff). Stir in the apples, sultanas and nuts until evenly combined.

Transfer the mixture to the prepared tin and bake in the preheated oven for 1 hour. An inserted skewer should come out clean when cooked. Served hot or cold, it's great with cream or ice cream.

Irene in her new kitchen, 1958

AUNTY 'RENE'S CHICKEN & RICE

Reading through my great aunt Irene's recipes, many of them made use of tinned ingredients. This method of preserving food had been developed in the early 1800s by the French so that their army could have better quality food in the field. However, the process was labour intensive, costly and wasn't properly used in mass-production until the British army requested better food rations for their troops during the First World War .

This method of preserving rations made its way into food shops, providing the busy housewife with more choice with a whole host of recipes being developed to make use of the different ingredients available in tins. Its simple convenience and the fact that you didn't need to worry about it going off in a hurry made tinned food a big hit with consumers and its popularity is still strong today.

This recipe is one that I've eaten when over visiting my family a few years back. It's so simple to throw together to cook and perfect if you're busy, as you can make it and leave it to bake while you carry on doing something else. There's nothing wrong with tinned food at all and you can enjoy this simple chicken and rice dish with some vegetables or a simple salad as a great midweek meal for the family.

SERVES 4-6

4 boneless and skinless
   chicken breasts

250ml milk

75g crispy onions

100g white rice

1 tin mushroom soup

1 tin leek and potato soup

prep: 10 minutes, cook: 2 hours

Preheat the oven to 160°C fan/180°C/gas mark 4.

In an oven proof dish measuring 32cm x 23cm/ 9 inch x 13 inch, stir the two different tinned soups together with the milk.

Sprinkle in the rice and add the chicken. Finish by sprinkling the crispy onions over everything and cover the whole dish tightly with foil.

Bake in the preheated oven for 2 hours and don't be tempted to peek as you will let the steam escape. Serve with some green vegetables or a fresh green salad.

NAN'S CORNED BEEF PIE

A staple main meal of wartime Britain, the corned beef pie was a comforting and filling supper for all the family. I've used a couple more ingredients than would have been used and twice the amount of pastry. Nan says that she would never have wasted butter in the pastry and would have made it all with lard – so it's up to you how you make the pastry. You can use leftover roast beef in the pie in place of the corned beef if you want to – make the recipe yours to enjoy, however if you have a tin of corned beef in the cupboard you can make the pie any time you fancy it.

Rations also would have corned beef hash as an option for the troops to eat and is slightly easier to make than the pie. Just parboil the potatoes and fry them with the onion until you get some delicious crunchy bits. Add the beef to warm through and enjoy with a fried egg.

SERVES 6

3-4 big potatoes

butter and milk for the mash

2 onions, chopped

1-2 tbsp of oil

1 heaped tsp dried sage

1 200g tin corned beef, roughly chopped

salt and pepper to taste

Pastry

250g plain flour

pinch of salt

60g butter

60g lard

prep: 30 minutes, cook: up to 30 minutes

Make the pastry by rubbing the butter and lard into the flour and salt until the mixture looks like breadcrumbs. Add tablespoons of water gradually until the mixture comes together to form a ball of dough. Tip out onto a floured surface and knead a little to bring it together. Wrap in greaseproof paper and chill in the fridge while you make the filling.

Make some mash by peeling, chopping and cooking the potatoes in salted water. Bring to the boil and reduce to simmer, cooking for about 20 minutes until they're soft. Drain and add a good knob of butter, a splash of milk and mash until smooth.

While the potatoes are cooking, chop and lightly fry the onions in a little oil over a medium heat until soft. Add the dried sage for the last couple of minutes then add to the mash along with the corned beef. Mix everything together – leaving some of the beef slightly chunky. Taste to check the seasoning, adding salt and pepper if required. I like lots of pepper!

Preheat the oven to 180°C fan/200°C/gas mark 6 and grease a metal pie plate. Divide the dough and roll one half out on a lightly floured surface to about the thickness of a pound coin. Carefully lift it and line the pie plate, making sure it fits snugly to the plate and has a little pastry over-hanging the edges. Fill the plate with the beef and mash mixture, shaping the filling so that it's evenly spread. Roll out the remaining pastry to the same thickness. Using a beaten egg, brush the edges of the filled pastry before lifting the top onto the pie, pressing around the edges to seal.

Trim any excess pastry from the pie and crimp the edges with your fingers, a fork or a piping nozzle. Brush the rest of the egg wash over the pie and pierce the top to let the steam escape as it cooks. Feel free to decorate the pie or leave plain and simple.

Bake in the preheated oven for about 25-30 minutes, until the pastry is golden brown. Serve hot or cold.

NAN'S RISSOLES

If you're looking for a no-frills recipe to make the most of any Sunday lunch leftovers, you can't beat rissoles. The ingredients list is vague when it comes to items and quantities – if you had any leftover potato then you could add that into the mix or make a bubble & squeak with the vegetables to serve with the meat rissoles.

Nan often made them when we were young – nothing went to waste and I was in awe of both my grandmothers who could make something delicious to eat from what looked like hardly any ingredients. Being able to open the fridge or a cupboard and create a meal to feed a family is definitely a skill and something that was common practice during rationing and both world wars. I find it hilarious when Nan tells me 'You'll never starve, Bec, you'll always make something out of nothing', – and it's all thanks to her.

Use any leftover cooked meat you have. There may not be a lot, but try and get as much off the bone as you can. Some recipes coat the rissoles in breadcrumbs, but Nan tutted at this practice. While researching at the Imperial War Museum, I came across a recipe for lentil rissoles which was equally as sparse when it came to the ingredients list. Bulking out the meat rissoles with some cooked lentils or beans would work well.

SERVES 4-6

meat left over from Sunday
   roast
onion roughly chopped
salt and pepper to taste
1 tsp dried herbs
1 egg
a handful of breadcrumbs
flour to dust
2 tbsp oil for frying

prep: 15 minutes, cook: 12 minutes

Mince or finely chop the meat with the onion and place into a medium bowl. Add a little seasoning and herbs to taste and stir to combine. Add enough egg and breadcrumbs to bind the mixture together. Divide into 4 or 8, depending on how much mixture you have, and with floured hands form into balls and flatten into patties. Place on a plate and chill in the fridge until ready to heat.

Heat the oil in a frying pan over a medium heat. Dust the patties in a little flour and fry in the oil until golden, turning a couple of times to get an even colour. You're not cooking the meat, just re-heating, so make sure they're hot before serving.

Eat with some vegetables, a salad or bubble & squeak and brown sauce.

NAN'S FISH CAKES

This recipe is a tasty meal made from store cupboard ingredients that's filling and quick to make. It's something that Nan would make for me and my brother if we were staying over for lunch and its simplicity is its strongpoint.

I remember Nan using either tinned tuna or salmon depending on what was in the cupboard. She'd usually have some leftover potatoes from the day before too, either boiled or already mashed. Nan grew up during a time when it wouldn't do to waste a single scrap of food, and this ethos was ingrained in her style of cooking and still persists to this day. This is one skill that I'm grateful to have picked up from both my grandmothers and my parents.

There's no reason why you can't use fresh fish. Just cook it first and flake the flesh into the mash as directed below. You can make the cakes ahead of time and keep them in the fridge until you're ready to cook them.

SERVES 4

1 large tin of tuna or salmon, roughly 120g weight (drained)

3 potatoes

1 tbsp butter

3 spring onions

1 tsp dried parsley or fresh parsley

salt and pepper

flour for dusting

1-2 tbsp oil

prep: 30 minutes, cook: 12 minutes

Peel, chop and cook the potatoes in salted water. Bring to the boil, reduce to a simmer and cook for about 20 minutes or until soft. Drain the potatoes and mash with the butter.

Chop the spring onions and fresh parsley and add to the mash along with the tuna and stir to combine. Taste and add salt and pepper if required.

Divide the mixture into 4 equal portions and with floured hands, lightly shape them into patties. Place the oil in a frying pan over a medium heat and carefully cook the fish cakes on both sides until golden brown.

Serve hot with vegetables. Peas are a good partner in my opinion. Salad is of course another great accompaniment.

Use any herbs that you have to hand, dried or fresh. Half an onion slightly fried would be a good alternative to spring onions too.

My grandparents, Nan and Dups

MAM-GU'S CAWL

Cawl is a Welsh institution. The word is often translated as 'soup'. But cawl is not just any soup, it's not even really a soup as such but more of a stew – and yet, it's not exactly a stew either, but don't let that confuse you – the ingredients are simple, and it's easy to cook the most delicious, comforting hot meal.

It was one of those meals that was made weekly by Mam-gu to feed Dat (my grandfather), six children, farm hands and anyone else who was on the farm. Often served on its own, it was a complete meal in a bowl. However some chunks of cheese and bread would be placed on the table to make sure that everyone left with a full belly.

Made using a fresh cut of meat – lamb, beef or ham – whichever was available and whatever vegetables were available, with water and salt and that was it. If there was meat left over from Sunday lunch, then that would be used in place of a fresh piece of meat. The broth that bubbled away in the pot would take on a sweet earthiness from the vegetables and an iron rich depth of flavour from the meat and bone.

To some it might be considered traditional and dated, but this, in its bare essence, is good honest food and something that stood the test of time during wartime Britain.

Mari and Mam making cawl

SERVES 6

1kg lamb shoulder, on the bone

5 large potatoes

3 carrots

1 swede

1 large leek

fresh parsley

salt and pepper

oil and butter

prep: 15 minutes, cook: up to 3½ hours

In a large saucepan place the meat and cover with water. Bring to the boil and reduce to a simmer, skimming off any scum that rises to the surface. The meat will take 2-3 hours to cook until tender and falling off the bone.

After this time, peel and chop the potatoes, swede and carrots to bite-sized pieces, add to the pot and season with salt and pepper. Simmer for 20 minutes before adding the sliced leeks and cooking for a further 10 minutes. Taste to check the seasoning and add some chopped parsley right at the end.

Just before serving, remove the meat and shred/chop into bite-sized pieces before returning to the pot. Serve in bowls with bread and cheese.

GRILLED MACKEREL & TOMATOES

My memories of Mam-gu are bittersweet. As the youngest of her grandchildren I was spoilt, however I wish I could have had more time with her. Any recollections of her are therefore very special.

Mam-gu was a petite lady, with chocolate brown eyes and a sharp wit. She was on the go from the moment she woke up until she went to bed again – apart from the 20-minute mid-afternoon cat nap she took on the sofa, mouth wide open catching flies whilst watching wrestling. She was a phenomenal female role model for me to be inspired by, especially when it came to her cookery skills.

She kept her knives in tip-top condition; they were so sharp that you could get a cut just by looking at them. She had this amazing knack of cutting everything wafer thin and most impressive was the way she cut bread for sandwiches; the slices were paper thin. She'd sit the loaf up on its short end, generously cover the cut side with some deliciously salty butter and then slice a piece off – it was like watching a magician – nothing short of mesmeric. One of her staple lunches was thinly sliced tomatoes from her garden, folded inside one wafer thin slice of bread and butter with a pinch of salt and a scalding hot mug of tea.

My parents often share stories of Mam-gu going to market to buy cockles, local sewin or mackerel for their lunch – no frills, just simple and honest. This recipe is just that: grilled mackerel with Dad's infamous tomato salad, thinly sliced, of course.

▲ Mam-gu and Dat's wedding,, c 1920

SERVES 4

4 fresh whole mackerel or 8 fillets

vegetable oil

salt and pepper

6 large tomatoes

1 red onion

white wine vinegar

olive oil

crusty bread

prep: 15 minutes, cook: 5 minutes

Start by making a tomato salad, as the fish will cook in minutes. Slice the tomatoes and red onion as thinly as possible and layer them in a bowl, alternating between the tomatoes and red onion. Season with some salt and drizzle over some oil and vinegar. Give a half-hearted stir to the dish, taste and adjust by adding more salt, vinegar or oil if needed. Leave to one side while you cook the mackerel.

If using whole mackerel, ask your fishmonger to gut the fish. If using fillets, allow 2 per person and be careful of bones. Heat the grill to high and rub both sides of the whole mackerel with oil and salt. Place on a baking tray and grill the fish for about 2-3 minutes on each side for the whole fish, 1-2 minutes for the skin side of the fillets and 30 seconds for the flesh. Alternatively you can pan fry the fish in a little oil, skin side down until golden, then flip to just cook through the flesh. Serve the mackerel hot from the grill with a wedge of lemon the tomato salad and crusty bread.

TRADITIONAL FRUIT CAKE

Three doors down from where Nan lived was Mrs Mowbray, whose son was in the RAF and, more impressively, the Dambusters. Whenever he came home, he brought gifts to his mother including dried fruit which Mrs Mowbray kept to give to Nan for her to use in her wedding cake.

My grandparents got married in 1947 with a beautiful cake (so I've been told), baked and decorated by my aunty Winnie. In 1973 she used the same cake tin to bake my parents' wedding cake. When my husband and I married in 2011, I baked the cake, using Aunty Winnie's recipe in the very same tin which has now served three generations of our family.

Here's my traditional fruit cake that I make every Christmas and for weddings. I often change what fruit I use, depending on what's in the cupboard and what I fancy. Brandy is the traditional tipple of choice. However, dark, spiced rum works beautifully with all the sweet dried fruit and spices.

MAKES ONE 20CM/8-INCH ROUND CAKE

200g dried cranberries

200g currants

200g sultanas

200g raisins

75g candied or mixed peel

125g glace/candied cherries

7-8 tbsp brandy/rum/sherry/ whatever you fancy

1½ tbsp treacle

zest of 1½ small lemons

zest of 1½ small oranges

juice of 1 small orange

225g butter

225g brown sugar

4 eggs

225g plain flour

1½ tsp mixed spice

1 tsp ground nutmeg

1 tsp ground cinnamon

40g ground almonds

60g slivered almonds

prep: 30 minutes, cook: up to 4½ hours

Preheat the oven to 130°C fan/150°C/gas mark 2. Grease and line a deep 20cm/8-inch cake tin with two layers of greaseproof paper, making sure that the paper comes up higher than the height of the tin by at least an inch. I also wrap the outside of the tin with some newspaper and tie it with string; this gives the cake extra protection for the long slow bake. Put the tin to one side while you make the mixture.

You can soak the dried fruit in the brandy and orange juice overnight if you like, but if you forget, don't panic. Place all the dried fruit in a bowl and add the brandy, orange juice, zest and treacle. Give it a good stir and put to one side. Cream the butter and sugar together in a large bowl until light in colour. Gradually add the eggs then the flour and spices until thoroughly combined.

Add the ground and slivered almonds to the mixture along with the fruit and brandy and give everything a good stir. We tend to get everyone in the house to stir the cake at this point and then pack the whole mixture into the cake tin. It may look like it won't fit, but have faith – it will. Make sure you press the mixture down as you're filling the tin, ensuring there are no air holes. Smooth the top and then lightly cover the cake with a round of greased greaseproof paper with a small hole in the middle for you to test later with a skewer.

Place in the oven on the middle shelf and bake for 3½-4½ hours. The cake is ready when an inserted skewer comes out clean. Once baked, leave the cake to rest on a cooling rack. I tend to bake the cake in the afternoon and leave it to cool under a tea towel overnight. Once completely cool, gently remove from the tin and give it a feed of brandy, about 1-2 tbsp should do the trick. Wrap it in double greaseproof paper and then double foil and place in a tin. (It will

'sweat' in a plastic Tupperware box.) Keep it somewhere cool and feed regularly. I tend to make the cake at least 3 months ahead of the big day, just so that it has longer to mature and take on more brandy!

Decorate to suit your style and age group. I always cover the cake with marzipan and icing ahead of adding any decorations.

MAM-GU'S BARA BRITH

Staying on the theme of dried fruit, I wanted to share Mam-gu's recipe for Bara Brith, a type of fruit loaf incorporating dried fruit in abundance, that would have been made much more regularly than a traditional fruit cake, especially in Wales. A beautifully simple tea loaf, Bara Brith is a teatime staple in Wales, made using strong tea and best served with a thick layer of salted Welsh butter.

MAKES 1 LOAF

55g soft butter

225g self-raising flour

145ml strong tea (use 2-3 tea bags)

115g brown sugar

1 tsp bicarbonate of soda

1 egg

pinch of salt

225g mixed dried fruit

¼ tsp mixed spice

prep: 15 minutes, cook: up to 1hour and 10 minutes

Preheat the oven to 130°C fan/150°C/gas mark 2 and grease and line a 450g/1lb loaf tin.

Place the butter, sugar and fruit into a mixing bowl and add the bicarbonate of soda and salt. Add the strong tea and mix well. Add the beaten egg and fold in the flour and mixed spice.

Pour the mixture into the prepared tin and cook for 1 hour and 10 minutes. Leave to cool completely in the tin. Serve with salted butter or with some blue cheese slightly warmed on top with a drizzle of honey.

TIPS:

You can glaze the finished loaf with some marmalade and toasted seeds and nuts.

Make two and freeze one, then you can enjoy a slice when you fancy it.

Bara Brith freezes well – wrap it in greaseproof paper and then place in a large sandwich bag or Tupperware box. Alternatively keep in an airtight tin.

MAM-GU'S APPLE DUMPLINGS

This is a family recipe from Mam's farming side and a firm favourite with everyone. Essentially, it's a simple apple pie, but in our family we call them apple dumplings. Baked apples were a popular recipe during wartime Britain, as apples were readily available. You can keep the recipe nice and simple and not have the pastry, but then that would mean that you're not eating apple dumplings. We have a tradition in our family of eating puddings with milk rather than cream, and Dad informs me that this is due to when they would have milk as children, the top part of the pint would be a thick cream – much like Jersey Gold Top.

SERVES 4

4 cooking apples

6 tbsp brown sugar

4 tbsp sultanas/raisins

2 tsp mixed spice

½ quantity of the pastry from Nan's Corned Beef Pie recipe, page 18

milk to glaze

prep: 25 minutes, cook: 30 minutes

Make the pastry and leave to chill while you prepare the apples.

Preheat the oven to 180°C fan/200°C/gas mark 6 and line a baking tray with greaseproof paper.

Wash and dry the apples and remove the core. If you don't have a corer, use a sharp knife; Mam-gu never had a gadget to core an apple on the farm – that's for sure!

In a small bowl, mix together 4 tablespoons of the sugar, the sultanas or raisins and the mixed spice. You can also add some chopped nuts or any other dried fruit if you fancy. Some orange zest and juice is a nice addition – or a glug of whiskey.

Roll out the pastry to about 5mm thick on a floured surface and cut it into 4 pieces. Place an apple in the middle of one of the pastry pieces and wrap the dough up and around the apple, making sure not to cover the top and the hole. Repeat with the remaining 3 apples and place all 4 onto the lined baking tray.

Fill the apples with the sugar and sultana. Brush the pastry with the milk and sprinkle the remaining 2 tablespoons of sugar over the pastry.

Bake the apples in the oven for about 30 minutes or until the pastry is golden brown and the apples are soft.

Serve hot with cream – or like our family, with milk.

CHAPTER 2

COOKHOUSE CLASSICS

An army chef might be called upon to cook meals for troops in field kitchens in any situation anywhere in the world. The same cook might rustle up a weekend brunch, a midweek apple crumble or turn their hand to cooking up a storm for mess functions or regimental dinners. Being versatile is just one aspect of these talented and skilful chefs.

The humble cookhouse is nothing more than a school or office canteen, but when you're living on camps, it's your kitchen and dining room and after a long day you hope for something filling and comforting to be on offer on the supper menu.

The chefs know what type of food will please the troops – classics like cottage pie or chicken Kiev – and if you're lucky you may have a Gurkha chef in the kitchen who will whip up a stonking curry once a week too.

There are also themed nights that the chefs like to put on to help break up the monotony of the menus that they have to cook. Some are big hits like Mexican or Chinese night.

The chefs know that the meals they cook are more than fuel for the troops who live on camp; they know that they miss being with their families or that they might be young and newly joined and are homesick, and so it's even more important that the food they have on offer includes dishes that will provide that home comfort as well as being nutritious and balanced.

SERGEANT'S MESS BRUNCH

Brunch is that wonderful meal served usually on the weekend, best enjoyed in the company of good friends. It seems that anything goes when it comes to the dishes on a brunch menu, from a traditional fry-up to something a bit more global like Huevos Rancheros – a firm favourite of mine when served with plenty of chilli. However, I do love a hash brown, but not from the freezer section. The best I've tasted was when I was in Texas as a little girl – the potato was grated along with some onion and fried, so that you had some proper crunchy bits. So simple, and yet so delicious.

Another brunch classic is eggy bread. Now in our house, we eat our eggy bread with ketchup, however you can eat it with icing sugar, cinnamon and syrup and call it French toast. I remember learning how to make eggy bread when I was at Brownie camp as a little girl. Unsurprisingly I spent a lot of time in the kitchen with the Brownie leaders helping them prepare our meals, and when I went home, I wowed my family with this delicious fried bread dipped in egg. I often make it as a quick lunch for myself, especially if there are some ends of bread that need eating as stale bread works well in this way.

Brunch is a regular mealtime on the weekends in the forces too, with eggy bread being a staple on the menu alongside everything else you could possibly want to eat. Basically, brunch can be a combination of your favourite breakfast and lunch items all on one plate, and so here's my ideal brunch for you to enjoy with friends and family on the weekend.

SERVES 4

ONION & POTATO RÖSTI

500g potatoes – something like a Desirée

1 large or 2 medium onions

40g butter, melted

salt to season

EGGY BREAD

4 eggs

a splash of milk

salt and pepper

4 slices of bread

1 tbsp oil

a knob of butter

200g cherry vine tomatoes

300g mushrooms

1 tbsp oil

salt and pepper

8 rashers of smoked streaky bacon

prep: 30 minutes, cook: 50 minutes

Preheat the oven to 200°C fan/220°C/gas mark 7. Peel the potatoes and cook in a saucepan of salted boiling water for about 6-8 minutes. Drain the water and once they're cool enough to handle, grate the potatoes and the onion and place them in a bowl. Drizzle over the melted butter, season with salt and mix well so that everything is glistening.

On a lined baking tray, spoon the mixture into 12 heaped mounds and press down gently. Bake in the oven for about 40 minutes, or until crunchy and golden.

Cut the tomatoes and mushrooms into quarters and place them on a separate baking tray. Drizzle with oil and season with salt then bake in the oven for the last 15 minutes of the röstis' cooking time.

For the eggy bread, beat the eggs, add a splash of milk and salt and pepper and place into a shallow bowl – I use a pasta bowl. Slice the bread thickly – like a doorstop. Heat ½ the oil and butter in a frying pan over a medium heat. Dip 2 slices of bread into the egg, making sure both of them get a good dunking. Fry the first 2 slices in the oil and butter for a few minutes until golden, then flip to cook the other side. Keep warm in the oven while you do the same with the remaining slices.

Finally – grill the bacon or dry fry until crispy and serve. I like to have a glass of orange juice with brunch and plenty of ketchup. Alternatively, you could serve everything with my homemade beans from page 64.

Brunch with my best friends Beth & Emily

GOAT CURRY & AFGHANI BREAD

My husband has been posted operationally to Afghanistan twice. The first time was before we'd met and during the conflict in 2007. He was with the Grenadier Guards and experienced a type of warfare never before witnessed. We don't talk too much about that tour as he was injured badly on the front line and had to be medevacked back to the UK for surgery on his leg and hand. His body armour saved his life.

We met the month after he had returned and was still reeling from his experiences out in Afghanistan. He lost good friends during that tour and he himself suffered with pain in his hand and leg and had deep mental scars like many who have fought on the front line.

His recent tour was with the Royal Army Medical Corps on NATO peacekeeping duties. My concerns about him going out caused me great anxiety, as I didn't want him to suffer mentally, having done so well with his recovery over the previous few years. The situation in Afghanistan had changed greatly and he truly benefited from going out there to revisit the areas where his experiences had changed him both physically and mentally.

All things considered, it's funny that the main topic of conversation about his tour in 2007 is food and memories of the most amazing goat curry he has ever tasted. To honour his time spent in Afghanistan, I wanted to include this recipe so that it would remind him of the good times.

SERVES 6

600g lamb leg or goat, chopped into cubes

5cm ginger, grated

4 garlic cloves minced/grated

4½ tbsp white vinegar

¾ tsp ground black pepper

1 tsp salt

5 tbsp oil

¾ tsp whole black peppercorns

1 tbsp coriander seeds

1 tbsp cumin seeds

2 whole dry red chillies

4 fresh green chillies

fresh coriander for garnish

6 large tomatoes

prep: 30 minutes, cook: 1 hour

In a medium bowl, mix the ginger, garlic, vinegar, black pepper, oil and half the salt (½ tsp). Add the cubed meat, mix well and leave to marinade for about 3 hours.

Meanwhile toast the spices: black peppercorns, coriander, cumin and dried chillies until they start to pop and release their aroma. Then grind them in a pestle and mortar or coffee/spice grinder.

Remove the skin from the tomatoes by scoring a cross on the bottom of each one before submerging them in a bowl of boiling water for about 30-60 seconds. Carefully remove the skin and roughly chop the tomatoes, the coriander and chillies.

Add the oil to a hot pan along with the meat and brown for 5 minutes, stirring occasionally. Then reduce the heat to low, cover and cook for 30 minutes, stirring every so often. After this time, add the chopped tomatoes and continue to cook for a further 20-25 minutes.

Next, turn the heat up to medium-high and add the remaining ½ tsp salt, the toasted ground spices and chopped chillies. Give everything a good stir and leave to bubble until the sauce has thickened. Sprinkle the coriander over and serve.

If you don't fancy goat, then lamb will work just as well.

AFGHANI BREAD

AFGHANI BREAD

400g strong white bread flour

145ml lukewarm water

4g fast acting yeast

½ tbsp sugar

½ tbsp salt

2 tbsp vegetable oil

1 tbsp milk

AFGHANI BREAD

Mix 70ml of the water with the yeast and sugar and leave to bloom for 10 minutes. The yeast should appear frothy when it's ready to use.

Put the flour in a large mixing bowl, add the salt and give it a quick stir. Make a well in the middle and add the frothy yeast mixture and the oil. Mix everything, adding the remaining water and knead until you have a soft dough. Smooth over a small amount of oil, place back in the bowl and leave to rise for 1-2 hours or until double in size.

Once it has doubled in size, divide the dough into 4 equal balls. Using a rolling pin, roll each ball of dough into an oval shape, measuring roughly 15cm long and between 1-2cm thick. Place the rolled-out dough on lined baking trays and mark it using a fork to create lines across the width of the bread, about 2cm apart. This is decorative but also helps to stops the bread puffing up while baking.

Leave the dough to prove again for 15 minutes. Preheat the oven to 200°C fan/220°C/gas mark 7. After the second prove, brush the top of the breads with milk and bake for 10 minutes, or until golden brown and serve hot with the goat curry.

PORK WELLINGTON

Beef Wellington is a dish that I've eaten pretty much at every regimental dinner, mess function or dine-out and I can understand why. It's one of those dishes that shouts pomp and ceremony. It was named for Arthur Wellesley, the 1st Duke of Wellington to celebrate his triumph over Napoleon Bonaparte at the battle of Waterloo. It is also said that the dish was an English version of Bœuf en Croûte, with other similar dishes being created during the same period of history – essentially it's a posh pie.

I remember watching Dad making this dish for the first time at home. He was slightly stressed, making sure that the meat was cooked and that the pastry wasn't soggy. Despite the anxiety, it always tasted amazing. I especially loved the mushroom and red wine sauce he made to go along with it.

To honour my husband's service to the army I thought I would make this posh pie using his favourite meat, pork, as the centrepiece in a slight twist to tradition, but still keeping true to its roots.

SERVES 4-6

1 large pork fillet

2 tbsp oil

20g butter

salt and pepper

5-6 slices Parma ham

1 tbsp Dijon mustard

1 small onion, finely sliced

2 garlic cloves, grated/crushed

150g chestnut mushrooms, finely chopped

2 sprigs fresh thyme, leaves removed

1 Granny Smith apple, grated

300g puff pastry or homemade rough puff (page 105)

flour for dusting and rolling

1 egg to glaze

prep: 40 minutes, cook: 45 minutes

In a large frying pan heat a tablespoon of oil, season the meat all over with salt and pepper and brown in the pan, adding a teaspoon of butter at the end. Remove the meat and leave to rest and cool. Keep all the delicious meat juices for the mushroom gravy.

In another frying pan, heat the remaining oil and butter and sweat the onions, garlic, mushrooms and thyme with a pinch of salt and a little pepper until soft. Add the grated apple at the end and cook to evaporate some of the moisture. Taste to check the seasoning then remove to cool.

On a lightly floured work surface, roll out the pastry into a rectangle slightly longer than the pork fillet and at least 3 times wider so that the pastry will completely cover the fillet and all its stuffing. Lay and overlap the Parma ham onto the rolled-out pastry and then spread the Dijon mustard on top. Cover this with the mushroom and apple stuffing, then place the cooled pork fillet on top. Carefully roll the pastry up and over the pork fillet, so that the ends slightly overlap and form a seam. Trim any excess off the sides and fold these in too so that the pork fillet is completely sealed within the pastry, Parma ham and stuffing.

Carefully lift the Wellington onto a lined baking tray and glaze with a beaten egg, before chilling in the fridge for an hour. Preheat the oven to 180°C fan/200°C/gas mark 6 and brush the Wellington again with more egg glaze. Using a sharp knife, score the pastry with neat diagonal lines along the length of the Wellington before baking it in the oven for 30-35 minutes or until golden. Leave to stand for 10 minutes before slicing.

MUSHROOM GRAVY

30g dried mushrooms

2 shallots, finely sliced

1 garlic clove, grated/crushed

a glug of port or red wine

1 tsp redcurrant jelly

300ml vegetable stock

1 tsp Marmite

1-2 tsp cornflour to thicken

While the meat is cooking, make the gravy by soaking the dry mushrooms in some just boiled water for 20 minutes. Add the finely chopped shallots and garlic to the pan that was used to cook the meat and sauté gently over a low heat until soft. Roughly chop the soaked mushrooms and add to the pan, keeping the mushroom water to use later. Turn up the heat after a couple of minutes, add the port or wine and scrape any goodness off the bottom of the pan. Add the mushroom water, stock redcurrant jelly and Marmite. Bring to the boil and reduce to a simmer, leaving it to bubble away and thicken. When ready to serve, taste to check the seasoning and add a little cornflour mixed with water to thicken if needed.

Serve the pork Wellington with your choice of greens, potatoes and some of the mushroom gravy.

CRISPY CHILLI CHICKEN & EGG FRIED RICE

During Matt's recent tour of Afghanistan, I was, of course, concerned with what he was eating. Was he getting enough food? Was it tasty … ? I needn't have worried, especially when Matt mentioned that the chefs were from Sri Lanka – I knew he would be enjoying some full-flavoured meals.

I take my hat off to all those men and women who work in the cookhouses, chow halls and field kitchens.

'An army marches on its stomach' means more than just eating for fuel – yes, they need to have the energy to carry out their duties abroad and at home, but do not underestimate the energy a good meal will give you, both physically and mentally. Matt looked forward to this meal every Sunday – and little moments like that, make being away from home and family a little bit more bearable.

Matt on a blackhawk helicopter in Afghanistan, 2019

SERVES 4-5

4 chicken breasts

60g plain flour

60g cornflour

salt and pepper

3 tbsp vegetable oil

1 tbsp sesame oil

2 garlic cloves

1 thumb-sized piece of ginger

1 onion

1 carrot

2 peppers

1 fresh chilli

1-2 tbsp soy sauce

4 tbsp ketchup

½ tbsp honey

juice of ½ lime

2 spring onions to garnish

prep: 25 minutes, cook: 20 minutes

Place the rice into a saucepan along with 400ml of water and a good pinch of salt. Bring to the boil, cover and reduce to simmer for 8-10 minutes. Then turn the heat off and leave the pan with the lid on.

Prepare the vegetables for the chilli chicken; thinly slice or julienne the ginger, carrot, onion and pepper and place to one side. In a bowl, mix together the plain flour and cornflour and season with salt and pepper. Cut the chicken into strips and coat in the seasoned flour. In a frying pan, heat 2 tablespoons of the oil over a medium-high heat and fry the chicken until crispy. Once cooked, place on some kitchen roll on a plate to soak up any excess oil.

Clean the frying pan by carefully wiping it with some more kitchen roll, then return to the heat and add the remaining tablespoon of vegetable oil and a tablespoon of sesame oil. Stir-fry the ginger, onion, carrot and pepper for a few minutes before adding the garlic and chilli. Add the soy sauce, ketchup, honey and a splash of water and leave to bubble and thicken for a couple of minutes.

FOR THE RICE

200g white rice

2-3 garlic cloves, crushed

2 eggs

100g peas

2 spring onions

salt

Add the chicken and stir. Finish with a squeeze of lime and some chopped spring onions.

To make the egg fried rice, place some oil in a separate frying pan over a medium heat and stir-fry the garlic and peas for a minute. Add the cooked rice and stir to combine. Move the rice to the outside of the pan and crack the eggs into the middle. Leave them for 30 seconds so that they start to cook before stirring through the rice. Season with salt or a little soy sauce and finish with some chopped spring onions stirred through.

Serve the crispy chilli chicken with the egg fried rice – the ultimate homemade take-away meal.

MAC 'N' CHEESE

Macaroni and cheese is a favourite meal in the American services chow halls as well as in ration packs. It's an institution that is devoured by adults and children across America and I can understand why. Pasta and cheese? Yes please. It's comfort food that's packed full of energy for the troops, which makes it a perfect dish to serve to them.

The Ministry of Food promoted a version of this classic in its Cookery Calendar leaflet series during post-war Britain in 1949. The recipe doesn't have much cheese in it but is packed with tomatoes and carrots mixed with macaroni pasta and has a cheese topping.

This recipe would have suited the rationing that continued into the late 1940s and the early 1950s, using vegetables to bulk out meals and little or no meat. Cheese was used only as a topping due to the small ration that a person could claim each week, although vegetarians would have slightly more instead of their meat ration.

Mac 'n' cheese was the first (and only) dish that my husband made for me when we started dating and I was mightily impressed that he could make a delicious cheese sauce from scratch. Here's my version which is jam-packed with cheese. I've added some mustard and jalapeño peppers for a kick and suggested some vegetable and meat additions should you fancy them.

SERVES 4-6

3 tbsp butter

3 tbsp plain flour

500ml milk

1 garlic clove, grated

1 white onion, chopped

½ tbsp mustard powder

50g jalapeño peppers (jarred), roughly chopped

1 small tin of sweetcorn, drained

150g mature Cheddar cheese

75g Gruyère cheese

50g Parmesan cheese

50g full fat cream cheese

400g dried pasta macaroni

salt to taste

a good handful of crispy salad onions

prep: 25 minutes, cook 20 minutes

Heat the milk in a saucepan and add the grated garlic and chopped onion. Bring the milk to just below boiling then turn off the heat.

Cook the pasta in salted water until it's nearly ready, drain and keep to one side while you make the sauce.

In another saucepan melt the butter over a medium heat, then add the flour and mustard powder and stir with a whisk to combine. Add the warmed milk a little at a time to make a thick white sauce.

Reduce the heat and add the cream, Gruyère and Cheddar cheeses and stir until melted – taste to check the seasoning. Add the sweetcorn, chopped jalapeño peppers and pasta and stir to combine. Taste again to check the seasoning, then transfer to a large oven dish.

Sprinkle on the grated Parmesan cheese and crunchy salad onions and bake in a preheated oven set to 180°C fan/200°C/gas mark 6 for 20 minutes or until golden brown.

Enjoy as a main dish with salad or as a side dish to some barbecued meat.

TIP:

This is a vegetarian dish and is perfect as it is – however, feel free to add crispy smoked bacon or leftover roast chicken if you have any. Also, vegetables like peas, chopped peppers and tomatoes or roast carrots/sweet potatoes are a good addition. My husband likes to add some soft-boiled eggs, hidden underneath the pasta as a treat to find when you dig in.

CHICKEN KIEV WITH RATATOUILLE & ROSEMARY ROASTIES

This chapter was named Cookhouse classics for a reason, and it could be epitomised by this recipe. You can't beat a chicken Kiev for supper after a long day on duty, especially when it's served with chunky chips and peas. It's a rather nostalgic dish for those who grew up in the 1970s and 1980s – but has recently enjoyed a return to glory in gastropubs up and down the country.

I'm pairing this classic with another: the humble ratatouille, and rather than chunky oven chips – which I have nothing against and always have a bag of them in the freezer – how about some rosemary roasties? Not the usual Sunday roast crunchies, but some rustic skin-on tasty cubes of potatoes. I also like to use Japanese panko breadcrumbs for the Kievs as they add a good crunch and colour beautifully whilst cooking, but homemade breadcrumbs will do just as well.

SERVES 4

4 chicken breasts

175g breadcrumbs

2 large eggs

75g plain flour

2-3 tbsp vegetable oil

½ tsp each of smoked paprika, cayenne pepper, cumin and dried thyme

salt and pepper

3 large garlic cloves

small bunch of chives, parsley and tarragon, finely chopped

100g unsalted butter, soft

squeeze of lemon

RATATOUILLE

2 tbsp olive oil

1 courgette

1 small aubergine

2 onions, white or red

2 peppers – any colour you fancy

5 garlic cloves

1 tin tomatoes

2 tsp smoked paprika

salt and pepper

prep: 40 minutes, cook: 45 minutes

Start by making the garlic butter for the middle of the Kiev. Place the soft butter in a bowl and add grated or crushed garlic and the chopped herbs. Season and mix well using a fork. Scrape the mixture into some cling film, wrap it up and shape it into a fat sausage shape then pop it into the fridge or better still, into the freezer for at least an hour.

For the chicken, place the breadcrumbs on a plate, crack the two eggs into a bowl and beat with a pinch of salt. Place the flour on another plate with the spices, thyme, salt and pepper and mix together.

Cut a pocket into each of the chicken breasts using a sharp knife. Cut the chilled garlic and herb butter into 4 equal slices and carefully insert one into each of the chicken breasts. The butter should sit right in the middle of the breasts, with none protruding. Press together to seal the parcels.

Dip the chicken in the seasoned flour, then into the egg and then finally into the breadcrumbs. Double dip the breast into the egg and breadcrumbs again so that the Kievs are extra crunchy. Once all breasts are coated, place them on a plate and chill in the fridge.

Preheat the oven to 190°C fan/210°C/gas mark 6-7. Wash the potatoes and roughly chop them into 2-3cm/1-inch cubes, keeping the skin on. Place into a baking tray and drizzle over the oil and some salt. Toss the potatoes in the oil and salt, add the sprigs of rosemary and garlic cloves. Roast in the oven for 45 minutes, turning halfway.

For the ratatouille, roughly chop all the vegetables into bite-sized pieces. Heat the oil in a large pan with a lid and start by cooking the

ROSEMARY ROASTIES

5 large potatoes

5 sprigs of rosemary

2-3 tbsp olive oil

5-7 garlic cloves, skins on

onions for a couple of minutes. Next add the courgette, aubergine, pepper and garlic, stir and cook for a further 5 minutes with the lid on, stirring occasionally. After this time, add the smoked paprika, tinned tomatoes and some seasoning. Reduce the heat to a simmer, pop the lid on and let the ratatouille cook gently for about half an hour or until the vegetables are super soft.

To cook the Kievs, preheat the oven to 160°C fan/180°C/gas mark 4. Heat 1½ tbsp of oil in a large frying pan and cook 2 of the breasts for a couple of minutes on each side until golden. Remove from the heat and place on some kitchen paper while you repeat with the other chicken breasts. Bake in the oven for 25 minutes.

Serve the chicken Kiev with the rosemary roast potatoes and the soft and smoky ratatouille.

CLASSIC COTTAGE PIE

The classic cottage pie may not be the sexiest option on the menu, it's more like a faithful friend that you can always rely on to be there and never let you down. It's a dish that features often in the cookhouse, especially during the winter months. It's pretty much a complete meal in itself, and best of all you can eat it with just a fork.

With its crispy, buttery and comforting mash enveloping the rich stew-like mince underneath, you can see why this dish is a staple for the troops as it's tasty and filling and provides energy and nutrients.

Cottage pie and its cousin, the humble shepherd's pie, will always remind me of Ben, my flatmate in London. We would host dinner parties where the menu would almost always include one of these pies, some great company and lots of wine. I have very fond memories of my time living with Ben and it was an honour making the cake for his and Bex's wedding – and the main meal at their reception was shepherd's pie.

SERVES 4-6

1 tbsp olive oil

1 large onion

1 large carrot

2 celery sticks

400g lean beef mince

100g red lentils

100g green lentils

2 tbsp tomato purée

1 tbsp plain flour

1 tsp dried thyme

a good glug of red wine

500ml beef stock

Worcestershire sauce and soy sauce to taste

salt and pepper to season

950g Maris Piper potatoes

65g butter

4 tbsp milk

prep: 30 minutes, cook: 45 minutes

Heat the oil in a large pan over a high heat and add the mince – don't be tempted to stir for a couple of minutes until the meat starts to colour and caramelise. While the meat is browning, finely chop the onion and celery, peel and finely chop the carrot, then add to the meat and stir, turning the heat down to medium. Add a pinch of salt and pop a lid on so that the vegetables can sweat and soften. After about 8 minutes of sweating and occasional stirring, add the lentils and thyme followed by the tomato purée. Stir and cook for a couple of minutes.

Sprinkle over the flour. Stir, then add a good glug of wine and cook for 2 minutes before adding the stock. Give everything a good stir and then add the Worcestershire sauce and soy sauce to taste. Reduce the heat so that the mixture is simmering and leave to bubble away quietly and thicken for about 30 minutes.

Peel and chop the potatoes into halves or quarters and bring to the boil in salted water. Turn the heat down and simmer for 15 minutes until tender. Drain and mash the potatoes with the butter and milk until smooth. Taste and season as required. Preheat the grill ready to crisp the top before serving.

Once the mince is cooked and thickened, spoon the mixture into an oven-proof dish and top with the mash, spreading out gently to cover and using a spoon or a fork to create small peaks which will catch and crisp under the grill. Finish by grilling the pie for about 6-8 minutes, or until suitably crunchy on top. Serve with your choice of vegetables.

BAKED BLUEBERRY CHEESECAKE

It may surprise you to know that I don't have a sweet tooth. Instead of a cake covered in buttercream, I much prefer something savoury like a freshly baked loaf of bread or a meat pie any day. There are of course a couple of exceptions to this rule. I go weak at the knees for anything creamy like a chocolate éclair, tiramisu or cheesecake, especially one that's baked. I love strong flavours too, like a sharp tarte au citron or bitter dark chocolate and a strong and punchy black coffee. If something is too sweet, then it just overpowers any other flavours or ingredients that may be present in the dish.

It's very easy to buy a poor quality cheesecake – one that's got hardly any filling, too sweet, or has blatantly just been put in the fridge to set. When I want cheesecake it has to be baked, which admittedly takes a little more effort, but cheesecake is a treat so I don't mind pushing the boat out every so often. The problem is that I will inevitably have to share it with others, something I'm not very good at doing when it comes to food in general, but especially with chocolate éclairs and baked cheesecakes.

I knew I'd married a keeper when we found we agreed on all the merits of a cheesecake. He would reminisce about the cheesecakes he had in the cookhouse when he first joined the army, stating that the best ones were either fruits of the forest or orange flavoured. For me, you can't beat a classic plain vanilla cheesecake, however, serving it with a simple blueberry sauce is just divine – and don't get me started on how delicious a Snickers version is – all that peanut, caramel and chocolate goodness in cheesecake form is just too much for my brain and taste buds to cope with.

Here's my plain vanilla baked cheesecake recipe for you to try with a simple blueberry sauce. As an alternative you could gently melt a couple of Snickers bars to drizzle on top and add some chopped toasted peanuts for extra crunch – and I give you permission to not share this with anyone else!

SERVES 8-10

150g Oreo biscuits

65g butter, melted

½ tbsp caster sugar

FILLING

900g full-fat soft cheese

250g caster sugar

45g plain flour

a good pinch of salt

¾ tbsp vanilla extract or vanilla bean paste

3 large eggs

1 egg yolk

200ml sour cream

prep: 30 minutes, cook: 1 hour

Preheat the oven to 160°C fan/180°C/gas mark 4 and grease and line a 23cm/9-inch loose-bottomed, springform tin. Blitz the Oreo biscuits into crumbs then add the sugar and melted butter and stir. Pour the mixture into the prepared tin and press down with the back of a spoon to form an even base. Bake in the oven for 10 minutes then remove the base, place aside and increase the oven temperature to 200°C fan/220°C/gas mark 7.

Place the cream cheese in a large bowl and beat using a wooden spoon or an electric hand whisk until smooth. Next, gradually add the sugar, followed by the flour and salt. While still whisking, add the vanilla extract and the eggs. Finally add the sour cream and whisk until just combined. Pour the mixture on top of the base, bursting any bubbles with a sharp knife, then bake in the oven for 10 minutes.

Reduce the oven temperature to 90°C fan/110°C/gas mark ½ and continue to bake for 50 minutes. Leave the cheesecake in the oven

BLUEBERRY SAUCE

300g blueberries

zest and juice of ½ lemon

1-2 tbsp caster sugar to
   sweeten

1 tsp of cornflour

to cool, with the door open for 2 hours and don't worry if the top cracks slightly.

While the cheesecake cools, make the blueberry sauce by placing the blueberries, lemon zest and juice and however much sugar you need, along with a splash of water into a pan and gently heat, stirring occasionally until the blueberries have started to burst. Mix the cornflour with a drizzle of water and add to the pan to thicken the sauce.

You can serve the sauce warm or cold with a good wedge of the cheesecake.

WELSH WONDER – CHEESY LEEK TART

There's a tradition in The Royal Welsh regiment of wearing leeks on St David's Day, and also eating the leeks – raw! I'd heard of this tradition from other wives whose partners were with the Royal Welsh, but when my husband started a job in Wales as a permanent staff instructor with a reserves unit; they also had a tradition on St David's Day to get any new members of staff or recruits to eat a raw leek. Let's just say he was happy that he only had to do it once as an initiation and not every St David's Day.

In honour of this tradition, here's a delicious tart celebrating the leek in all its glory. It's a light and refreshing dish, perfect for lunch or supper served with a fresh and peppery watercress salad. I'm cheating slightly by using shop-bought puff pastry, but you can, of course, make rough puff pastry if you prefer. (See recipe page 105)

SERVES 6

1 tbsp oil

a knob of butter

4 large leeks

250g ricotta cheese

75g Parmesan cheese, grated

100g baby leaf spinach

zest of 1 lemon

salt and pepper to season

300g ready-made puff pastry,
    either rolled or in block form

prep: 25 minutes, cook: 30 minutes

Wash and thinly slice the leeks. Heat the oil in a medium pan and sauté the leeks with a good pinch of salt over a gentle heat until soft. Pop the lid on so that the leeks sweat, stirring occasionally so that they don't catch on the bottom of the pan. They should take about 10 minutes to cook until soft. Taste to check the seasoning, adding salt and pepper if needed. Remove from the heat.

Meanwhile, add the butter, spinach and a drop of water to a medium saucepan over a medium heat. Stir and pop a lid on to wilt the spinach. After 1-2 minutes remove from the heat, drain away the liquid and leave the spinach to cool.

Preheat the oven to 180°C fan/200°C/gas mark 6 and roll out the pastry onto a greased or lined baking tray and bake in the oven for about 10 minutes. While the pastry is cooking, put the cooled spinach into a bowl along with the ricotta and 50g of the Parmesan cheese. Add the lemon zest, taste and season with salt and pepper.

Once the pastry has baked for 10 minutes, remove it from the oven and fully press down the middle, leaving a 1cm border all the way around. Spread the ricotta and spinach mixture evenly from the middle, right up to the border. Add an even layer of the leeks and sprinkle over the remaining Parmesan cheese.

Pop the tart back into the oven and cook for a further 8-10 minutes. Serve with a watercress salad.

COMFORTING PUDDINGS WITH CUSTARD

What is it about old school puddings that are now being considered comfort food? Rice pudding, apple crumble, jam roly-poly, not forgetting custard, which was an intrinsic partner in crime accompanying whatever delicious pudding was being served.

BAKED JAM ROLL

Jam roly-poly is such a simple pudding to make and can be flavoured with whatever jam you have in your cupboard. My husband reminisces about the strawberry flavoured jam roll he had during his basic training, and I'm surprised that he had enough time to taste or even remember it considering that, as he says, it was during basic training that he perfected his skill of eating food at a rapid rate of knots.

I prefer cherry or blackcurrant jam, but any jam or marmalade would work. And you can serve the jam roll with cream or ice cream, of course, but in order to fully step back in time to that school pudding comfort memory, then custard must be served.

SERVES 8

butter to grease

230g self-raising flour

a good pinch of salt

110g suet

120-140ml milk

4 tbsp of your preferred jam

1 egg

3-4 tbsp caster sugar and demerara sugar mixed

CUSTARD

500ml whole milk

6 egg yolks

75g caster sugar

1 vanilla pod or 1 tsp vanilla bean paste

½ tbsp cornflour to thicken

prep: 20 minutes, cook: 35 minutes

Preheat the oven to 180°C fan/200°C/gas mark 6 and grease a large baking tray with the butter.

In a large mixing bowl mix the flour, salt and suet until combined. Using a rounded knife to stir, add the milk a little at a time until a ball of dough forms that's not too sticky or too dry. On a lightly floured worktop knead then roll the dough out into a rectangle measuring about 20cm x 30cm.

Spread the jam over the dough, making sure to leave a little border – about 1cm wide the whole way around. Roll up the dough from the long side to form a Swiss roll, sealing the edges gently. Place the jam roll, seam side down onto the buttered baking tray. Beat the egg and use to glaze the roll all over, and then sprinkle it with the mixed caster and demerara sugars. Bake in the oven for 35 minutes, or until golden brown.

While the jam roll is baking, make the custard. Heat the milk and vanilla in a medium pan until just below boiling, then remove from the heat. Whisk the egg whites and caster sugar until combined then add the cornflour and whisk. Carefully add the milk little by little, whisking continuously until it has all been incorporated. Pour the mixture back into the saucepan and heat gently, stirring until the custard has thickened.

APPLE & BLACKBERRY CRUMBLE

Fruit crumble is another pudding that gives you a big old hug and manages to warm every part of your body. Mam-gu would make an exceptional rhubarb crumble, but called it cherry-apple as my brother and I told her we didn't like rhubarb!

My apple and blackberry crumble uses eating apples so that there's some good bite to the fruit portion of the crumble, coupled with crunchy oats and nuts on top to add a good balance of texture. And if you don't serve the crumble with custard, well there's just no hope is there?

SERVES 8

50g butter
50g light-brown sugar
450g eating apples
½ tsp ground ginger
½ tsp ground cinnamon
160g blackberries

CRUNCHY CRUMBLE TOPPING

150g plain flour
80g unsalted butter
80g light-brown sugar
30g flaked almonds
30g rolled oats

prep: 25 minutes, cook: 30 minutes

Peel, core and chop the apples into 2cm cubes and place into a medium saucepan along with 50g of butter, 50g light-brown sugar and the spices. Gently melt the butter and sugar, stirring the mixture occasionally for about 5 minutes then add the blackberries and cook for a further 2 minutes, before removing from the heat.

Preheat the oven to 180°C fan/200°C/gas mark 6.

To make the crumble, place the flour, sugar and unsalted butter into a bowl and lightly rub the ingredients together to form breadcrumbs. Add the flaked almonds and oats and stir to combine.

Pour the fruit into an oven proof dish and top with the crumble mixture. Bake in the oven for 30 minutes or until the topping is golden. Serve hot with custard.

CHAPTER 3

RATIONS REINVENTED

Rations have played a big part in the diet of all military personnel but haven't always been well received. Modern-day 24-hour ration packs are a well-balanced box, ensuring that the individual gets about 4,000 calories, giving them enough energy to carry out their duties. The boxes are filled with meals and snacks that can be eaten hot or cold and also have hot and cold drinks in the form of powdered sachets.

There's an impressive variety of dishes and any number of diets are catered for, so it's a comfort to know that your loved one has food that is tasty and giving them the energy that they need.

I love the little touches that are also included in the boxes, like a packet of tissues and a small bottle of Tabasco sauce for those who wish to add a little spice to their lunch. There's always the ritual of exchanging different meals with others if you 'get unlucky' and find your least favourite meal in the box – there's always someone there who will happily swap with you.

Then there's the utter indulgence of the chefs being nearby, cooking in the field kitchen, meaning that lunch is going to be hot rations and not something that you have to heat yourself. It's these meals that keep you going – literally. The restored energy, the short rest, and the mental uplift allow the troops to keep on doing their jobs.

I've taken inspiration from some classic ration pack menus as well as what the awesome chefs manage to make while out in a tent in all conditions, and hopefully these recipes will bring joy and comfort to you and plenty of energy to keep you going.

RANGE STEW

I often hear stories of meals that my husband has eaten while out on the army training area, more so when they've been treated to hot rations as these tend to really give them all a boost while out in the field, especially in bad weather. Matt went all nostalgic as he retold the story of when he had his first ever range stew …

It was during his basic training phase, while on his second exercise out on the training area near Deepcut and it tonked it down (that's raining ridiculously heavily in army speak). The army chefs training centre was based nearby in Pirbright and unbeknown to them the trainee chefs arrived and set up a 12 by 12 with a cook set number 5 – which is army speak for a big tent and field kitchen – and started to prepare lunch. They proceeded to whip up hot rations of range stew and pasta shells for them all to wolf down at lunch.

Apparently, it was the best pasta Bolognese Matt has ever eaten and I can see just why he would think that. The army chefs were like guardian angels in disguise, appearing out of nowhere through the storm, setting up their field kitchen and cooking a feast, before clearing up and moving on again. Army chefs – you're all legends. Thank you for feeding our troops, regardless of where you are and what is going on around you.

You hear 'stew' and you think chunky vegetables and meat in a broth or gravy of some kind, but range stew is actually a generic term used to describe any kind of hot stew-like dish, which could be Bolognese, or chicken in white sauce or mince with veg, or … I could go on. It's not a specific dish, but an affectionate term used to describe the hot meal that they have on the range that day. It's also known as range slop!

Here's a versatile recipe for beef mince and vegetables that can be eaten with pasta, rice, mash or used to stuff baked peppers – the essence of range stew; warming, filling and adaptable.

SERVES 6-8

2 tbsp oil

500g beef mince

1 large onion, roughly chopped

1 large or 2 medium carrots, peeled and roughly chopped

1½ tbsp plain flour

1 tin tomatoes

soy sauce

Worcestershire sauce

1 beef stock cube

200g garden peas

salt and pepper

prep: 15 minutes, cook: 40 minutes

Heat the oil in a large saucepan over a medium heat and add the chopped onion. Sweat for a few minutes until soft, stirring occasionally. Move the onion to the side of the pan, turn up the heat and add the beef mince. Leave until the meat starts to colour then stir the mixture.

Cook for a few minutes then add the chopped carrot and the flour and stir. Next add the tinned tomatoes. Stir and bring to the boil. Add a few dashes each of the soy sauce and Worcestershire sauce, then add the beef stock and bring back to the boil, before reducing to a simmer for about 20 minutes, stirring occasionally until the liquid has reduced a little. Taste to check the seasoning. Add the peas for the last 5 minutes and then serve.

Serve the mince with some potatoes and other vegetables, with pasta and cheese, rice, or fill peppers with the mixture, cover with cheese and bake in the oven. Add chilli flakes if you fancy a bit more of a kick. This can also be used as a pie filling.

JAM DOUGHNUTS

Believe it or not, my husband informs me that range stew was always accompanied with half a frozen jam doughnut. Now I'm not too sure on how accurate this is, especially the frozen bit, but I believe my husband, of course.

Regardless of its authenticity, a jam-filled doughnut is a very welcome sight as a dessert when you're cold and wet out on the training area doing another bone (pointless) exercise. Below is a classic doughnut recipe with a homemade raspberry jam filling. I've made the dough without eggs and not too much sugar, plus a mix of water and milk in order to have a light dough to fry. An alternative filling is crème pâtissière – splendid vanilla or smooth chocolate. Both recipes are included because I'm good like that.

MAKES 16 DOUGHNUTS

500g strong white bread flour

10g yeast

10g salt

50g caster sugar

25g soft butter

120ml milk

200ml water

1 litre sunflower oil

150g caster sugar to dust doughnuts once cooked and cooled.

RASPBERRY JAM

250g fresh or frozen raspberries

250g jam sugar

juice of ½ lemon

prep: 40 minutes, cook: 30 minutes

Rub the butter into the flour, then add the yeast, salt and sugar and mix well. Add the milk and water and knead into a soft elastic dough. This will take about 8-10 minutes. Cover and leave to prove for roughly 2 hours, until doubled in size.

Make the jam by placing the raspberries, sugar and lemon juice into a large pan over a medium heat. The fruit will break down gradually and the sugar will dissolve. Once the liquid is clear of any sugar granules, increase the heat so that the mixture is bubbling and leave for a couple of minutes, stirring occasionally so that it doesn't stick.

To test if the jam is ready, drop a teaspoon full of the hot mixture onto a plate, leave for 20 seconds and then drag your finger through it. If the mixture wrinkles and holds its shape, then the jam is ready. If it's still liquid, then return to the heat for another minute or so and test again. Once set, remove from the heat to cool.

After proving, tip the dough out onto a lightly floured surface and roll until 2cm thick. Using a floured large round cutter measuring 4-5cm in diameter, cut out thick round shapes of dough. Collect the trimmings to re-roll and cut more doughnut shapes. Place them on a baking tray lined with greaseproof paper, covered with a tea towel for about 30-45 minutes, to prove a second time.

Add the oil to a medium-large pan and heat to 180°C. Test this with either a jam/sugar thermometer or by adding little pieces of bread to check – the oil will shimmer in the heat and if you add a piece of bread, it will fizz and turn golden.

Add the balls of dough in batches and fry until golden; this will take roughly 3-4 minutes each side. Drain on kitchen roll before dusting in sugar then fill them by piping the homemade jam into the middle, through a small hole in the side made with a skewer. Best served slightly warm and on the same day they're made.

CRÈME PÂTISSIÈRE

500ml full fat milk

6 medium free-range egg yolks

80g caster sugar

20g cornflour

20g plain flour

1 vanilla pod or 1 tsp vanilla bean paste

150g chocolate (optional)

Heat the milk with the vanilla pod until it just reaches boiling point. While the milk is warming, mix the egg yolks, sugar and flours together in a large bowl until pale. Remove the vanilla pod and gradually add the milk to the egg mixture and whisk continuously until all the milk has been added. Transfer the mixture back to the saucepan and bring to the boil, letting it bubble a little and stirring constantly. Transfer the mixture to a clean bowl and cover with cling film so as not to let a skin form. Place it in the fridge for a few hours to cool completely.

For a chocolate crème pâtissière, add 150g of melted chocolate to the mixture and stir before leaving it to cool in the fridge (as above).

BEANS & BURGERS

Beans on toast is one of those meals that never fails to satisfy, and the best thing is it's quick to make. It's a childhood staple that has stayed with me into adulthood and although I love the tinned variety, homemade baked beans are easy to make and so very tasty. I always make more than I need and freeze some in individual portions that I can defrost and heat up whenever I fancy. Served on toast is of course the classic way to eat beans or as a filling in a jacket potato, but they're equally as delicious served with rice and some green vegetables as a great vegetarian or vegan main meal.

In a ration pack, the baked beans are usually served with chicken sausages or burgers, and, as I'm sure you can imagine, this is a favourite dish amongst the troops and a great hot breakfast to have when it's cold out on the army training area.

I've not made normal beef burgers here but used a mix of beef and pork mince and added some fennel, chilli and garlic to add a bit of oomph to the dish. I've made mini burgers so that you can have more than one – but feel free to make bigger sized burgers if you want, just check that they're cooked thoroughly before serving.

SERVES 4-6

1 tbsp olive oil

1 onion

1 medium carrot

⅓ courgette

1 garlic clove, grated

1 tsp smoked paprika

½ tsp ground cumin

150ml passata

salt and white pepper

1 tin haricot beans, drained

1 tin cannellini beans, drained

BURGERS

200g beef mince

200g pork mince

1 small onion, finely chopped

1 garlic clove, grated

salt and pepper

1 tbsp fennel seeds

1 tsp chilli flakes

2 tbsp oil

prep: 30 minutes, cook: 40 minutes

Start by making the burger mixture. Gently fry the onion and garlic in a tablespoon of oil, for 6-8 minutes until soft. Place both minces in a bowl along with the onion and garlic mixture and the remaining ingredients, then use your hands to mix everything. Divide the mixture into 16 and roll into little meatballs. Place on a plate and keep covered in the fridge for 20 minutes.

To make the beans, peel and finely chop the carrot and onion, finely chop the courgette and grate the garlic. Heat the oil in a medium saucepan and lightly fry the onion and carrot for about 5 minutes, stirring occasionally. Add the courgette and garlic and cook for a further couple of minutes, before adding the paprika, cumin and passata. Give everything a good stir and add some seasoning. Reduce the heat and leave to simmer for 5 minutes.

Add both types of beans, stir to combine and cook for 8-10 minutes over a gentle heat. Taste to check the seasoning, adding more if required. The beans can be served straight away, cooled and reheated or frozen at this stage..

To cook the burgers, heat the remaining tablespoon of oil in a large frying pan over a medium heat. Cook the burgers in 2 batches; add the first 8 meatballs to the pan and leave to colour for 1-2 minutes, before squashing each meatball into a burger shape. Continue to cook for another couple of minutes, before flipping and cooking the other side until brown. Make sure the burgers are cooked through. Keep them warm in the oven at a low temperature while you cook the second batch.

Serve with
your choice of
potato or some
crusty bread
to mop up the
bean juice.

MEAT STICKS & RICE

I know that the title of this recipe may not sound that appetising but, apparently, it's a well-loved ration pack pouch and so I had to investigate further. I had visions of lamb koftas with rice and vegetables, but after a little research I discovered that the meat sticks are 50/50 beef/pork and that the brown rice is jam-packed full of vegetables, and plenty of herbs and spice for added flavour – it's no surprise really that this dish is so popular amongst the troops. Quite simply, it's tasty and filling and when you're out and about dining on ration pouches, it's always a treat to have one of your favourites ready to be warmed up and eaten.

I've tried to recreate the original dish so as to give you an idea of why meat sticks and rice is so tasty. You can, of course, use whatever vegetables you have, or even change the meat used in the sticks. Chicken mince would make them lighter, or you could use lamb mince.

SERVES 6

250g beef mince
250g pork mince
1 small onion
2 garlic cloves
1 tbsp olive oil
salt and white pepper

RICE

250g brown rice
600ml vegetable stock
1½ tbsp olive oil
3 garlic cloves
2 carrots
4 sticks celery
2 red peppers
150g runner beans
100g sweetcorn
100g peas
2 tbsp tomato purée
1 heaped tsp paprika
1 tsp dried thyme
1 heaped tsp Marmite

prep: 25 minutes, cook: 45 minutes

Finely chop the onion and garlic and fry in the oil over a low to medium heat for 5-8 minutes until they're soft. Remove from the heat and leave to cool slightly. In a medium bowl add both the beef and pork mince, ½ teaspoon of white pepper and ¾ teaspoon of salt. Add the cooled onion and garlic and, using your hands, mix the meats together well.

Divide the mixture into 24 equal portions and shape them into short sticks by rolling them into balls and then into sausage shapes. Place the sticks onto a plate and leave in the fridge for 20 minutes to set firm.

For the rice, roughly chop the red pepper, celery carrots and garlic. Fry the vegetables in the oil over a medium heat in a large saucepan until they're soft and start to colour. Add the tomato purée, paprika and thyme and cook for a further 2 minutes. Add the rice, vegetable stock and Marmite. Bring to the boil then reduce the heat, cover and simmer for 15 minutes.

Preheat the oven to 170°C fan/190°C/gas mark 5 and bake the sticks for 20 minutes, until they've coloured and cooked through.

After the rice has simmered for 15 minutes, add the peas and sweetcorn and continue to cook with the lid on for a further 5 minutes, or until the rice is cooked and the stock has been absorbed.

Serve the meat sticks and rice hot, preferably out of a mess tin with a spork, but a plate with a knife and fork will also suffice.

D SHAPES

Packed lunch bags are affectionately known as 'Horror Bags' in the army. Very charming. It's essentially a sandwich, crisps, fruit and a drink – but every so often, they're filled with the tastiest hand warmer ever invented – Cornish pasties, or D shapes as they're known in the forces. Below you'll find a traditional filling as well as my spiced crab and pea pasties for something with a little more oomph. Treat your own troops to some tasty D shapes, delicious on their own or with a salad and perfect to take out and about.

CORNISH PASTIES

MAKES 6-8 PASTIES

400g strong white bread flour
100g butter
100g lard
¾ tsp salt
140ml cold water
325g beef skirt
250g potato, peeled and cubed
125g swede, peeled and cubed

prep: 30 minutes, cook: 50 minutes

In a large mixing bowl, use your fingers to lightly rub the butter, lard, flour and salt together until they resemble breadcrumbs. Add water gradually, using a butter knife to bring the mixture together. Knead the pastry until it becomes smooth and elastic. Wrap in cling film and leave to rest in the fridge for about 2 hours.

While the pastry is chilling, prepare the vegetables by peeling and chopping the potato, swede and onion into 1cm cubes. Put them to one side in a bowl of water and cut the steak to a similar size.

125g onion, peeled and
chopped

salt and pepper to taste

1 egg to seal and glaze

Once the pastry has rested, roll it out to a thickness of 5mm and cut out round shapes using a side plate measuring about 20cm/8 inches in diameter.

Drain the vegetables, mix them with the steak and season well. Place some of the meat and vegetable mixture into the middle of the pastry rounds, brush a little egg on the edges of the pastry and bring them together and crimp to seal the filling inside.

Place the pasties onto a baking tray lined with greaseproof paper and glaze them with the beaten egg. Bake them in the middle of the oven at 170°C fan/190°C/gas mark 5 for about 50 minutes until golden. Serve warm.

SPICED CRAB & PEA PASTIES

MAKES 6-8 PASTIES

400g strong white bread flour

100g butter

100g lard

¾ tsp salt

140ml cold water

1 tbsp oil

1 knob of butter

1 onion, finely chopped

175g crème fraîche

2 tsp curry powder

550g white crabmeat

150g petits pois, defrosted

zest and juice of 1 lime

small bunch of coriander,
leaves and stalks chopped

1 fresh red chilli, finely
chopped – seeds in or out,
it's up to you.

salt to taste

quantity of shortcrust pastry

1 egg to seal and glaze

prep: 30 minutes, cook: 25 minutes

Make the pastry as described above and preheat the oven to 180°C fan/200°C/gas mark 6.

For the filling, heat the oil and butter in a frying pan over a low-medium heat and gently cook the chopped onion until soft. Remove from the heat and place in a large mixing bowl to cool.

In a small bowl, stir together the crème fraîche, curry powder and the zest and juice of the lime. Once the onions have cooled, add the crabmeat, defrosted peas, chopped coriander, chilli and the crème fraîche mixture and stir to combine. Season with a little salt and taste to check that you're happy.

Roll and cut out the pastry and divide the mixture between the pasties. Seal and glaze them as described above.

Bake the pasties on a baking tray lined with greaseproof paper for 20-25 minutes until golden brown. Serve warm with a fresh green salad.

FRUIT & NUT ENERGY BARS

Trail mix or energy bars are an integral part of a ration pack. They're one of the best portable snacks that packs a punch when it comes to energy When you're flagging and in need of a boost but are short of time, then one of these will definitely do the trick.

I've chosen dried fruit and nuts for colour, flavour and texture below, but feel free to use whatever fruit and nuts you prefer.

MAKES 12 BARS

340g oats

150g light-brown sugar

75g honey

80g coconut oil

80g butter

a good pinch of salt

75g dried apricots, roughly
    chopped

75g sultanas

75g dried cherries, halved

50g Brazil nuts, roughly
    chopped

50g hazelnuts, roughly
    chopped

prep: 15 minutes, cook: 25 minutes

Preheat the oven to 180°C fan/200°C/gas mark 6 and line a 23cm x 32cm/9-inch x 13-inch rectangular tin with greaseproof paper and set to one side.

In a large bowl, mix together the oats, sugar, salt, dried fruit and nuts. Melt the honey, butter and coconut oil over a low heat then add to the dry ingredients, making sure to mix thoroughly until evenly combined.

Scrape the mixture into the prepared tin and bake in the oven for 20-25 minutes, until golden brown. It's easier (and less messy) to leave it in the tin to cool completely before cutting into bars. Store in an air-tight container and eat within 5 days.

BISCUIT BROWNS

Which is your favourite ration pack staple, biscuit browns or biscuit fruits? This is a question that divides the forces and it's a sure-fire way to start a debate. My husband prefers the biscuit browns, essentially a cracker, which he enjoys with some pâté or peanut butter from the ration packs, but when I asked him about the biscuit fruits, he looked at me in disgust. He described them as Garibaldi biscuits, which, I think, are delicious, but he shuddered, saying that they were rock solid and not a patch on the biscuit browns.

Essentially, both biscuits are pocket-sized snacks to be eaten while you have a quick five-minute break on the training area. Biscuit fruits go well with your brew, and often the biscuit browns will have a handy, squeezy tube of pâté to enjoy as a rather frivolous topping to your savoury biscuits.

Biscuits were thought to be the original rations for sailors and soldiers alike due to the fact that they would keep for a long time, which is especially good if you're at sea. Give this recipe a try for a change to your usual cracker.

MAKES 16 BISCUITS

100g wholemeal flour
200g strong white bread flour
1 tsp dried yeast
1 tsp caster sugar
½ tsp bicarbonate of soda
½ tsp salt
130ml water
1 tbsp vegetable oil

prep: 25 minutes, cook: 12 minutes

Place the dry ingredients in a large mixing bowl and stir to combine.

Add the water and oil and mix to form a ball of dough. Knead on a work surface until smooth and pliable. Oil the mixing bowl and place the dough back into it. Cover and leave to prove for 1-2 hours.

Once proved, tip the dough out onto a lightly floured surface and roll it out to the thickness of a pound coin. Cut rectangle shapes measuring 8cm x 5cm and place them on a baking tray lined with greaseproof paper. Prick the biscuits evenly all over and leave to prove for another 30 minutes.

Preheat the oven to 200°C fan/220°C/gas mark 7 and bake the biscuits for 10-12 minutes. Leave to cool on a wire rack. Serve with pâté or some cheese and chilli sauce or chutney.

STEAMED SAUCY CHOCOLATE PUDDING

The humble steamed pudding is a rather simple thing, and yet it brings such warmth and comfort and can evoke wonderful memories of home and childhood.

If you find one in a ration pack sachet, you have struck gold. Imagine being out on the ranges in the cold and wet drizzle – weather often experienced on the Brecon Beacons – and you find a chocolate pudding in your pack. As soon as you get the chance, you are going to get that gas burner going in order to heat it up. You know it will warm and cheer you up enough to keep you going through the wet Welsh weather.

The only drawback with making a traditional steamed pudding at home is that it can take a long time to cook. The prospect of that prolonged wait until the heavenly moment when you can dive into that chocolatey bowl of goodness could end up putting you off making it in the first place. My microwave oven recipe is quick to make and comes with its own sauce, meaning you don't need to add anything to it or wait too long before you can enjoy it. Plus, it's all made and cooked in the same bowl, saving you time on the washing up too. It's a great dessert to whip up at the last minute and one that I'm sure will become a firm favourite.

SERVES 6-8

65g butter

225g self-raising flour

375g light-brown sugar

65g cocoa powder

185ml milk

1 tsp vanilla extract

TO SERVE

cream or ice cream

prep: 15 minutes, cook: 10 minutes

Melt the butter in a microwave oven in a 20cm/8-inches wide, deep ceramic microwaveable dish for about 40 seconds or until melted.

Sieve the flour and 30g of the cocoa powder onto the melted butter then add 200g of the light-brown sugar, the milk and vanilla extract and give everything a good stir to combine.

Sprinkle the remaining 175g of light-brown sugar and sieve the remaining 35g of cocoa powder on top, then pour in 300ml of boiling water. Do not stir, as these final ingredients create the sauce element of the pudding.

Place the dish back in the microwave and cook on high (800 watt) for 8 minutes.

Once cooked, leave the pudding to stand for a couple of minutes before serving.

MALAYSIAN MILKSHAKES

During the summer of 2001 I went travelling to Thailand and Malaysia with my best friend Beth. We were both twenty and couldn't wait to experience all that these two amazing countries had to offer. We spent the first half of our glorious holiday in Thailand, starting in Bangkok where, on the first night we watched the one and only Thai Tom Jones in performance! We travelled cross-country to some of the islands in the Andaman sea off the west coast before criss-crossing south on a mission to see the Perhentian islands off the north-east coast of Malaysia.

We had no ideas what to expect and having spent the last two weeks experiencing the bright lights of Thailand, we were hoping for a little desert island bliss to chill out and fully immerse ourselves in traveller life. We hopped off the boat onto a beautiful white beach with our rucksacks on our backs and headed towards a little cluster of huts gathered on one side of the beach. Our original plan was to stay for a couple of days, but we instantly fell in love with the island and decided to stay for five days … which was later extended to a week.

We spent our days mainly sunbathing until around 2pm, at which point we were usually in need of something to cool us down so we'd amble over to the same beachside bar – there were only a couple to choose from – and order a milkshake. Now, this wasn't any old milkshake. The first sip was out of this world and instantly cooled us down in the best, most refreshing way ever. My memory of the smooth, sweet, creamy, ice-cold glass of goodness has stayed with me all these years and just one sip of this recipe instantly transports me to that small island and that amazing summer spent on the other side of the world with my best friend.

My husband also had similar milkshake experiences when off-duty in Iraq. Once again, it was the long, deep cooling effect which was desirable after putting in a shift in such hot temperatures. Who'd have thought we'd have so many things in common? Even milkshakes.

The ingredients are few and the method is simple; the key being the condensed milk and plenty of ice. Use fresh fruit or your favourite chocolate bar – in my case that's mango and Malteser. It's best drunk on a beach with a bestie. Failing that – find a nice spot in the sun with some chilled-out tunes, preferably Bob Marley or David Gray. Their songs were always blaring out from our island beachside bar.

MAKES 1 MILKSHAKE

90g chopped fruit – fresh
    or frozen, strawberries,
    bananas, mango, etc.

handful of ice cubes

150ml milk

2-3 tbsp condensed milk

prep: 5 minutes

Place all the ingredients into a smoothie maker and blitz until smooth. Serve in a tall glass with a paper straw.

DAD'S MARMALADE RICE PUDDING

Rice pudding reminds me of a perfect Sunday, of having a lie-in, reading the papers, eating a delicious Sunday roast cooked by Mam and then having Dad's rice pudding to finish. I was always stuffed to the gills after the roast dinner but could always make space for rice pudding. In its purest form of rice, milk and sugar it has an ability to wrap its arms around you and fill you with love and warmth. And by adding a wee dram of whiskey and some marmalade, it's giving you one heck of a good kiss on the lips too.

Rice pudding is always popular in ration packs. It's easily heated or can be eaten cold, depending on where you are. It's sweet, warm and there's a decent amount in the pack to eat and fill you up. Some even get a little creative with their rice pudding and add their hot chocolate sachet to make it chocolatey, or their peanut butter ration to add more flavour. It's meant to be a pudding, but some have been known to have it for breakfast, which I could do quite happily, although maybe not with whiskey before the school run!

Here's a slight twist to the traditional version with the addition of some spice in the shape of a cinnamon stick and some saffron – these add warmth and colour and finally there's the marmalade and whiskey, for added tang and oomph.

SERVES 2

55g pudding rice

350ml whole milk

zest of 1 orange

1 stick cinnamon

a good pinch of saffron

1 tbsp light-brown sugar

110ml single cream

2 tbsp marmalade

a glug of whiskey (optional)

50g flaked almonds, toasted

prep: 15 minutes, cook 1 hour

Place the rice, milk, zest, cinnamon, saffron and sugar in a saucepan over a medium heat and bring to the boil. Reduce the heat, cover and cook for 1 hour, stirring occasionally.

When the rice is cooked, remove the cinnamon stick and add the cream, marmalade and optional whiskey and stir. Serve warm with a few scattered toasted almonds on top and a tot of whiskey on the side.

RATION PACK CHILLI SAUCE

The fact that ration packs come with their very own small bottle of Tabasco sauce makes me smile every time I think about it. It will instantly add flavour and a kick to whatever you're eating and give you extra warmth out on the training area too.

In honour of this delicious little fact, here's my quick and easy chilli sauce recipe. Don't be tempted to remove the seeds from the chillies before you make it otherwise what's the point of a chilli sauce? The hotter, the better if you ask me.

MAKES 500ML

4 bird's eye chillies, chopped

2 red chillies, chopped

3 garlic cloves, chopped

9 tomatoes, chopped

1 tbsp tomato purée

1 tsp sugar

a good pinch of salt

1½ tbsp oil

prep: 10 minutes, cook: 10 minutes

Heat a pan over a medium heat and add a little oil along with the tomatoes. Cook for a couple of minutes then add the remaining ingredients. Cook for a further 5 minutes then blend. This can be eaten hot or cold and stored in a sterilised jar or bottle in the fridge.

RUM SPIKED CRÊPES SUZETTE

During 1757, Dr James Lind conducted a radical experiment on some sailors. A ship's crew was divided into three groups and in addition to their daily diet, they were given a half pint of vinegar, a half pint of seawater or two oranges and one lemon. This ultimately proved that including citrus fruit in your diet was an effective way of warding off scurvy. During Cook's circumnavigation of the globe in 1772-75, he stopped the ship regularly to pick up fresh fruit and vegetables in order to avoid scurvy on board.

In 1804, the British Navy declared that lemon or lime juice would be added to the sailors' daily ration of grog to prevent them getting scurvy, with grog being the sailors' drink of watered down rum.

This story inspired me to make a twist on one of Churchill's favourite desserts, crêpes Suzette with the addition of rum in place of Grand Marnier as well as lime and lemon juice, just to make sure that I don't get scurvy of course!

SERVES 4-6

115g plain flour

pinch of salt

1 egg

290ml milk

butter for greasing

FOR THE SAUCE

3 tbsp caster sugar

200ml orange juice – from 2-3 oranges

zest of 1 orange

juice of 1 lime

juice of ½ lemon

50g unsalted butter

a good glug of rum.

prep: 15 minutes, cook: 30 minutes

Sift the flour into a bowl and add a pinch of salt. Crack the egg into the flour and begin to mix using a fork. Gradually add the milk, mixing well until it's all been incorporated. Leave to rest for 15 minutes while you prepare the ingredients for the sauce.

Place a frying pan over a medium heat and grease with a little butter. Pour a little of the batter into the pan and swirl the mixture around so that it coats the bottom of the pan.

Cook the pancake for about 2 minutes or until golden then flip using a palette knife or toss to turn over. Cook for a further 30 seconds to 1 minute then remove from the pan and fold into quarters and keep on a plate with greaseproof paper between each pancake. Repeat the process to cook more pancakes as required.

To make the sauce, pour the caster sugar into a non-stick frying pan and set over a low-medium heat. Let the sugar melt and turn a golden-amber colour – do not be tempted to stir the sugar, but you can shake the pan every so often.

As soon as the sugar has melted and turned amber, remove the pan from the heat and slowly add the orange juice, being careful not to get spattered with hot molten sugar. Add the orange zest, lime and lemon juice as well as the rum and stir over a low heat.

Add the butter gradually and simmer, stirring occasionally until the sauce has reduced slightly. Return the folded pancakes to the pan and warm through, coating them with the sauce.

Serve 2-3 pancakes per person, along with the sauce and a drizzle of cream if you fancy it!

Tip: You can add some segments of orange into the sauce if you wish

CHAPTER 4

KEEP THE HOME FIRES BURNING

Partners of military personnel are left on their own, often with children and a household to run, some juggle a day job too, with no family nearby to help.

With two young daughters to take care of, meal planning is a weekly activity; ensuring that there's food in the house for lunch boxes as well as for supper; often making sure that there's something quick to prepare and eat ahead of all the after-school activities.

Planning ahead, and making enough meals to freeze, means I can easily re-heat tasty food that I know the girls will eat. It's too easy to turn to convenience foods when you're busy, and even though I always have a bag of chips and some fish fingers in the freezer, just in case, most of the time I will get the girls to help cook something to eat.

I encourage them to think about what they want to eat, and we'll often research new dishes to try out. They're great at trying new foods and are always more than happy to help me in the kitchen. We often talk about what Dad might be eating, and the girls will request things that remind them of him – it's little things like this that make being apart from each other easier to manage, as well as being able to make a video call while the girls eat their breakfast.

I think it's also important to eat together as often as possible – a slight contradiction to my Solo suppers chapter I know, but I will do a mix of eating with the girls and ensuring that I have some me time too – the best of both worlds. The girls also love eating as a family and enjoy helping me set the table for us to eat together.

It's this element of normality that's important to maintain when one parent is away from home – for both your own sanity and also for the children's routine. It's important for them to learn that life carries on when one of you is away, and it's the routine and helping each other that makes it easier and possible to do. The girls are my own private support network, and it's because of them that I can cope without my partner.

These recipes are firm family favourites in our house. There are a few breakfast ideas, lunches and suppers to please your own little troops as well as the adults.

CHOCOLATE PORRIDGE

Poring over the menus at the Imperial War Museum made me realise that porridge had been a firm fixture on the armed forces' breakfast bill of fare for a couple of centuries. It's easy to understand why, with its complex carbohydrates giving the troops plenty of energy to keep them going. So it's no surprise to learn that porridge remains a constant in today's rations packs.

I've heard stories of how the troops try to add flavour to their porridge ration by throwing their hot chocolate sachet into the mix as well as a peanut butter sachet if they have one. Porridge has become trendy again on social media, with fans all over the world taking their time to carefully arrange their toppings in an attractive pattern before snapping a picture to share with their followers … and I for one am guilty of doing just this.

Porridge is a big favourite of mine – and my girls. A plain bowl of porridge sweetened with a banana has helped me through several marathons and never fails to get me going if I've got a busy day ahead. I usually only use water as a liquid with a splash of milk, however coconut milk adds a tropical richness, especially if served with some tropical fruits and warming spices like cardamom, turmeric and ginger. Chocolate porridge is also a big favourite in our house and I've shared the recipe, below.

SERVES 3

160g porridge oats

2 tbsp cocoa powder

1 tsp ground cinnamon

a good pinch of salt

1 tbsp honey

a splash of milk

TO SERVE

4 tbsp Greek yoghurt

toasted chopped nuts

fresh or frozen raspberries – a
 handful per bowl

a little extra honey to drizzle

a pinch of cinnamon per bowl

prep and cook: 8 minutes

Place the oats, cocoa powder, cinnamon and salt into a saucepan and cover with water. Warm on a medium heat, add the honey, stir to combine everything and leave to come up to a bubble.

As the oats heat up, they absorb the water and the porridge will thicken. Add a splash of milk to loosen the mixture slightly. Cook for a few minutes and then divide between 3 bowls.

Serve with a spoonful of yoghurt, some berries, nuts, a drizzle of honey and a pinch of cinnamon.

VEG BOX CAMPFIRE CHILLI

Chilli is probably the girls' favourite meal and I'm not sure if it's to do with the taste or because of all the 'bits' that I do to go with it. Much like I do with my solo suppers, when it comes to meals like chilli, curry and Mexican food, I like to make a fuss of the meal and the girls, plus it's fun to add extra flavours and textures to your dish.

While the chilli is bubbling and the rice is cooking, the girls and I are lined up next to each other chopping spring onions, grating cheese, mashing avocado then putting everything into individual bowls and setting the table ready to eat. I dish up the rice and chilli and then leave the rest to the girls. They always have a little of everything, and I can see that my style of finishing dishes off for photographs is rubbing off on them, as they carefully spoon on the sour cream and avocado and scatter just enough spring onions for both flavour and colour.

Cooking is a great activity and a fantastic way of bonding. By taking the time and care to prepare a meal and present it to a loved one you're showing them how much you love and care for them. By cooking meals like this chilli, that are full of different flavours, the girls are broadening their tastes, experiences and outlook on life. Food is more than fuel, it's love and a gateway to the world and all its adventures that are waiting for my two little explorers.

SERVES 6

2 aubergines

2 tbsp olive oil

1 onion

1 carrot

1 green pepper

4 garlic cloves

1 tin black beans

1 tin chopped tomatoes

40g dark chocolate

3 tbsp tomato purée

55g red lentils

20g dried mushrooms

1 fresh red chilli

1 tsp chilli powder

2 tsp dried oregano

3 tsp ground cumin

3 tsp smoked paprika

2 tsp ground coriander

1 stick cinnamon

600ml vegetable stock

salt and pepper to season

prep: 30 minutes, cook: 45 minutes

To start, scorch the aubergines. This is easy if you have a gas hob, otherwise you will achieve a similar effect by placing the aubergines under a grill, or better yet on a barbecue. I put a cooling rack over my gas hob and then place the aubergines directly onto the flame, turning until they're coloured all over. Put them aside to cool.

Soak the dried mushrooms in some hot water until soft – they'll need about 20 minutes. Then chop the onion, pepper and carrot relatively small and place in a large saucepan with the rapeseed oil. Sweat until soft for about 5-8 minutes. You can scorch the green pepper too if you want, then chop and add to the onion and carrot after they've sweated for 5 minutes.

TO SERVE

360g rice

100g grated Cheddar cheese

150g sour cream

1-2 fresh chillies

4 spring onions

1 avocado

juice of ½-1 lime

Next, add all the spices except the fresh chilli, then add the tomato purée, stir and cook for a couple of minutes. Chop the garlic and chilli and add to the pan along with the lentils and stir everything. Chop the mushrooms and add along with the mushroom water and the black beans. Add the tinned tomatoes and chocolate and give everything a good stir. Leave to simmer for 15 minutes, stirring occasionally.

Taste to check the seasoning and add salt and pepper as required. Cut the aubergine into relatively large pieces and add to the saucepan, being careful not to stir too vigorously as you want to try and keep the aubergine intact.

Cook the rice according to the packet instructions. Serve the chilli hot with the rice, some avocado mashed with lime juice and salt, a spoonful of sour cream, some grated cheese, chopped spring onions and slices of chilli. I also like to add chopped coriander and some tortilla chips on the side for added crunch and 'scoopage'.

CHEESY HAMMY EGGY

I've had it on good authority that a favourite lunchtime snack in the Royal Navy is something called Cheesy Hammy Eggy and is their version of a Welsh rarebit. A fellow military wife and ex-serving Royal Navy friend, Kim, wrote to me about the recipe, and although it's not fine dining (her exact words), it's comfort food, and when her husband is away, her children often ask for the dish so that they can be eating the same thing as their daddy.

As mentioned, the dish is similar to a Welsh rarebit but with ham hock, which goes crispy under the grill and is then served with a poached egg on top. Kim's son also likes to add some chilli sauce for added kick – a good suggestion and one that I also follow.

This dish goes to prove that food doesn't have to be overly complicated to provide that much needed hug or comfort to help soothe a soul that's missing someone. I love its simplicity and the fact that Kim's children eat it when their dad is away.

SERVES 4

4 slices of bread

160g strong Cheddar cheese

6 eggs

150g ham hock, cooked and shredded

a few splashes of Henderson's relish

½ tsp English mustard

salt and pepper

a splash of vinegar

prep: 15 minutes, cook: 10 minutes

Preheat the grill.

Grate the Cheddar cheese, place in a medium bowl, crack in 2 eggs and add the ham hock, relish and mustard. Add a little seasoning and mix well.

Place the bread under the grill and toast on one side.

Turn the bread over and divide the mixture between the 4 slices and return to the grill until golden, bubbling and crispy.

Poach 4 eggs in boiling water with a splash of vinegar for 2 minutes and 10 seconds.

Serve a slice of the toasted cheesy hammy, with the poached eggy on top – with or without chilli sauce, with a nice green salad on the side.

This is a perfect lunchtime dish served with some salad that will no doubt satisfy and soothe.

TOAD IN THE HOLE

Food has great power to comfort when we're feeling at our lowest, but also has the magic to cheer and nurture us. That's why so many of the recipes in this book are linked to comfort food, because they're associated with the joy and love that I've experienced in my life with family and dear friends.

When I cook these recipes for my daughters, especially when my husband is away, it's a way of sharing these experiences and showing how much I love them, in the hope that these memories, like flavours, will stay with them and get passed onto their children.

Toad in the hole is nothing fancy. It's halfway to making a Sunday roast, without splashing out on a joint of roasting meat. I think what makes it special is the Yorkshire pudding, which we usually only have with roast beef but was also given the nod of approval if we requested toad in the hole as children. I have fond memories of being excited when I knew we were having it as a midweek roast after school.

Everyone knows that the humble Yorkshire pudding is the king of the roast trimmings and the best thing about it is that it's made from a handful of simple ingredients. What I usually do is make extra puddings and freeze them along with the last drop of gravy to make a midweek roast for my girls, however making the real thing from scratch is a proper treat and never fails to put a smile on the family's faces. Serve with simple onion gravy, some mash or rosemary roasties (recipe page 46) and your choice of vegetables.

SERVES 4

6 good quality sausages

115g plain flour

1½ tsp salt

3 eggs

285ml milk

2 tbsp chopped fresh thyme

5-6 tbsp vegetable oil

ONION GRAVY

1 tbsp vegetable oil

1 large onion, cut in half and
  thinly sliced

1 tsp chopped fresh thyme

500ml stock, beef is best but
  you can use vegetable and
  add a tsp of Marmite

1-2 tsp cornflour to thicken

prep: 25 minutes, cook: 30 minutes

Place the flour, salt and chopped thyme in the bowl, add the eggs and mix using a fork. Gradually add the milk until you have a smooth thin batter. Leave to rest while you start to cook the sausages.

Preheat the oven to 210°C fan/230°C/gas mark 8. Place the oil in a skillet, (or a frying pan that can go into the oven) on the hob over a high heat and start to brown the sausages. Once they've got a bit of colour on them, carefully pour in the batter and place the pan straight into the preheated oven and bake for about 30 minutes, or until risen and golden brown.

To make the onion gravy, heat the oil in a medium frying pan and gently cook the onions. Add a pinch of salt to draw out the moisture and to help bring out the natural sugars so that the onions start to caramelise. Cook for about 10-15 minutes then add the stock and Marmite (optional) along with the fresh thyme. Cook the gravy gently, reducing the liquid and adding a teaspoon of cornflour to a drop of water and stirring through the gravy just before serving.

Serve the toad in the hole with the gravy and rosemary roast potatoes along with some peas or buttered cabbage.

MEATBALLS & CHAMP

This recipe is a staple in our house when the other half is away. It's tasty and comforting, plus the girls enjoy helping me mix and roll the meatballs. The quantity below is enough to feed the three of us twice over, which makes those midweek suppers much easier knowing you have something on stand-by in the freezer.

I sometimes add red wine to the sauce once the onion has sautéed and the purée has been added. This gives a certain richness to the dish. I serve the meatballs with some creamy champ and any leftovers can be re-heated with pasta.

Champ is an Irish potato dish that would often make an appearance on the menus in the cookhouses of the armed forces, especially the Irish regiments. The spring onion adds a mild onion flavour to the mash and is a comforting partner to the rich meatballs.

SERVES 6

3 slices of bread, without
    crusts

3½ tbsp milk

250g beef mince

250g pork mince

2-3 garlic cloves

2 tbsp fresh parsley, finely
    chopped, plus extra to serve

50g pitted black olives, finely
    chopped

1 egg

½ tsp smoked paprika

½ tsp dried oregano

½ tsp salt

2 tbsp olive oil

Sauce

2 tbsp olive oil

1 small onion, finely chopped

2 garlic cloves, crushed or
    minced

1 tbsp tomato purée

2 tsp smoked paprika

a good pinch of chilli flakes or
    powder

1 tin tomatoes

1 glass red wine (optional)

pinch of sugar

salt to taste

Champ

600g potatoes, Maris Piper

60g butter

a good splash of milk

salt and pepper to taste

6 spring onions

prep: 30 minutes, cook: 40 minutes

For the meatballs, tear the bread and pop into a medium mixing bowl with the milk. Stir until the bread has absorbed all the milk. Add the beef and pork mince, crushed garlic, finely chopped parsley, chopped olives, smoked paprika, oregano, salt and the egg. Use your hands to evenly combine the mixture. Divide this into about 24 meatballs, roughly the size of a ping-pong ball. You can refrigerate them at this point while you make the sauce.

To make the sauce, heat the oil in a pan, add the chopped onions and fry over a medium heat for about 5 minutes until soft. Add the garlic, paprika, chilli and tomato purée and cook for a couple of minutes, stirring occasionally. If adding red wine, pour a good glassful into the pan now and leave to cook out for a couple of minutes before adding the tinned tomatoes, salt and sugar. Stir to combine, bring to the boil and reduce to a simmer. Keep the sauce bubbling on a low heat to thicken slightly for about 15 minutes.

In a frying pan, heat the oil over a medium heat and place the meatballs in a circle around the edge. Don't overcrowd the pan. You will probably need to cook the meatballs in 2 batches. Once coloured on one side, turn them carefully every 1-2 minutes in order to get an even colour and then transfer them to the pan with the tomato sauce to finish cooking.

For the champ; peel, chop and cook the potatoes in boiling salted water for 20 minutes until soft. Drain and mash the potatoes with the butter and milk, tasting to check the seasoning. Add the chopped spring onions and serve with the meatballs and tomato sauce, sprinkled with some chopped fresh parsley. I usually serve with some green vegetables too, for added flavour and colour.

PESTO PASTA & PEAS

Pasta is a go-to meal for many these days, with pasta and pesto possibly being the easiest to throw together if you've got a jar in the cupboard and some dried pasta to hand. Many cookery books in the 1930s and through the Second World War published recipes using pasta, which may be a bit of a surprise to some. *The Joy of Cooking* by Irma S Rombauer is a very well-known cookery book and was first available in Britain at the end of the Second World War. The chapter introduction for *Starchy Foods*, including spaghetti, macaroni and noodles gives brief and to the point advice on what to do with them – my favourite comment suggesting that pasta would take a good deal of doctoring to make it palatable. I'm sure all Italians would strongly disagree.

Macaroni seems to be the most popular shape used and appears in many cookery books and recipes of that era. Below is my recipe for homemade pasta, which you can roll out using a rolling pin should you not have a pasta machine. You can easily cut the pasta into thin strips to make tagliatelle or spaghetti to enjoy with fresh and vibrant pesto. To add more substance to the dish, I add whatever vegetables I have to hand – which even includes peas from the freezer.

SERVES 2

200g '00' pasta flour

2 eggs

PESTO

a large bunch of basil, leaves
    and stalks

1 garlic clove

50g pine nuts

30g Parmesan cheese

120-150ml olive oil

salt and pepper

½ lemon

TO SERVE

150g petits pois

½ broccoli

25g Parmesan cheese, grated

prep: 20 minutes, cook: 10 minutes

For the pesto, place the basil, garlic and pine nuts in a food processor with a little of the olive oil and pulse into a rough paste. Grate the Parmesan cheese and add to the processor and, with the machine switched on, gradually add the oil until it reaches the desired consistency. Check the seasoning, adding salt and pepper to taste as well as a little lemon juice. Store in a jar in the fridge with a layer of olive oil on top.

For the pasta, place the flour and eggs in a large bowl. Using a fork, whisk the eggs to break them up and gradually pull on the flour to form a dough. Once the majority of the mixture has come together, tip out onto a clean work top and knead to work the gluten until the dough is smooth. This will take about 5 minutes. Once smooth, wrap in cling film and leave it to rest for at least 30 minutes.

To roll out the dough, a pasta machine is easier than rolling by hand, but using a rolling pin will do the same job – it will just take longer. Divide the dough into 3-4 pieces and flatten it to fit into the widest setting of the pasta machine. Pass the dough through, then change the setting down a notch and pass the dough through again. Fold the dough in half, go back up to the widest setting and pass the dough through again. Repeat this step a couple of times, then you can progress through the settings until you reach the thinnest setting. Fold the dough in half and then in half again and repeat back through the settings so that you have a smooth and thin dough.

If you don't have a pasta machine, use a rolling pin and be patient as it will take longer to roll the dough out thinly enough. Cut the dough into your preferred shape.

Cook the pasta, along with the broccoli and peas in boiling salted water for a couple of minutes, drain, add some of the pesto and stir. Serve with a little extra Parmesan cheese grated on top.

DAD'S SATURDAY MORNING WAFFLES

Dad used to work away a lot when we were growing up so we wouldn't see much of him during the week. This is similar to life in the forces if your partner lives and works away, only coming home on weekends – married/unaccompanied as they're called. However, Saturday mornings were special as Dad would be home and waffles were almost always on the menu to kick-start our weekend. This weekend treat has become a bit of a tradition now, with either waffles or pancakes whipped up for breakfast.

SERVES 4

250g self-raising flour

75g caster sugar

1 tsp baking powder

pinch of salt

3 eggs, separated

350ml milk

75g butter, melted

spray oil or a little extra butter
for greasing

TO SERVE

butter and syrup, maple/golden

crispy smoked bacon

fresh fruit and yoghurt

blueberry compote

prep: 15 minutes, cook: 20 minutes

Place the flour. Sugar, baking powder and salt into a large bowl and stir to combine.

Turn on the waffle machine according to the manufacturer's instruction. I heat mine to high and an indicator light turns green to let me know when it's ready.

Separate the eggs, adding the yolks to the milk and the whites into a medium mixing bowl. Mix the egg yolks and milk until combined and gradually add to the dry ingredients, stirring continuously until you have a smooth, slightly thick batter. Melt the butter and add to the batter.

Next, whisk the egg whites until they hold their shape and are stiff. Fold ⅓ of the whisked egg white into the batter using a spatula or a large metal spoon. Once fully incorporated, add another ⅓ and repeat the folding. Add the final ⅓ and carefully fold the mixture again until you have a light and aerated batter.

The waffle machine should be ready to go once you've made the mixture; carefully open the machine and grease the irons using a little butter on some greaseproof paper or use a little spray oil.

Ladle the mixture into the machine – my machine makes 2 squares of waffles which equates to 2 ladles of batter. Close the machine and cook until the indicator light illuminates again to let you know they're cooked; this is roughly 3-4 minutes.

Serve or keep warm in the oven until you've used up all the batter. The waffles can also be frozen and reheated/toasted when you want to eat them.

I enjoy my waffles with a little butter and syrup. They never last long on my plate and instantly take me back to being that little girl helping Dad make the waffles early on a Saturday morning.

Dad making waffles with Alys

OMELETTES, TWO-WAYS

Aren't omelettes great? You can have them any time of the day, with any ingredients you fancy – even a sweet omelette if you like. You can also make one to feed many or to just feed one, which is probably why I'm such a big fan. I like making omelettes for the girls because I know they'll devour them, but also happily help me choose and chop the ingredients. The best bit, of course, is cracking the eggs and trying very hard not to get any shell into the mixture, but a little added crunch every so often is fine with me.

Matt and I will often have an omelette for supper too. It's the perfect supper to enjoy when you're both tired and neither of you wants to cook as it's quick to make and very filling. I sometimes make an omelette just for me – one of my regular solo supper recipes that is also perfect for breakfast and lunch if the mood suits.

Here I share my daughter Alys's favourite omelette combination that we used to have nearly every lunchtime when Mari was in school and Alys was home with me. She loves the broccoli in the mixture and isn't the biggest fan of cheese, so only ever wants a small sprinkling in the pan.

I've also shared my favourite solo omelette recipe, which transports me back to our honeymoon and the amazing omelettes I had for breakfast. Be warned, this one has a good kick to it with plenty of chilli and coriander that is sure to wake you up and keep you going until lunchtime should you choose to have it for breakfast.

ALYS'S LUNCHTIME OMELETTE

SERVES 2

a knob of butter

½ tbsp olive oil

3 spring onions, roughly chopped

½ red pepper, roughly chopped

¼ broccoli head, roughly chopped

2 slices of smoked ham, cut into little squares

30g grated Cheddar cheese

salt and pepper

4 eggs

prep: 10 minutes, cook: 10 minutes

Chop all the ingredients and whisk the 4 eggs together in a small bowl with some salt and pepper. In a medium frying pan over a medium heat, add the butter and oil along with the spring onions, pepper, broccoli and ham. Stir-fry the ingredients for a couple of minutes until they colour a little and start to soften. Add the beaten eggs and leave for a minute to settle.

Using a fork or a spatula, carefully bring the edges of the omelette away from the sides of the pan, allowing some of the liquid mixture to fill the gaps and have its turn to cook. Continue the whole way around the pan until the majority of the mixture is setting.

Sprinkle the cheese over the top and let it melt a little before removing from the heat. Slide the omelette over to the side of the pan and fold it in half using a spatula. Divide the omelette between 2 plates and tuck in.

BECA'S SPICY BREAKFAST OMELETTE FOR ONE

SERVES 1

½ tbsp vegetable oil

¼ green pepper, finely chopped

½ red onion, finely chopped

1 medium tomato, finely chopped

1 bird's eye chilli finely chopped or 1 tsp of chilli flakes

handful of coriander, stalks and leaves all finely chopped

salt and pepper

2 eggs

prep: 10 minutes, cook: 10 minutes

Beat the eggs in a mug together with some salt and pepper. Place the oil in a small frying pan over a medium heat and add the pepper, onion, tomato and chilli. Stir-fry the vegetables for a couple of minutes until soft, then add the beaten eggs and chopped coriander.

Repeat the cooking method described above until the omelette is just set. Serve and eat immediately.

S'MORES COOKIES

S'mores are an American campfire classic, where you toast marshmallows on sticks until they scorch then you sandwich the hot sticky mess with some chocolate, between two Graham crackers and squish them together. The trick then is to eat the whole thing without burning yourself and getting melted chocolate and hot marshmallow everywhere.

Toasting marshmallows on a barbecue at the end of a meal or on an open campfire has become a tradition at summer gatherings and camping trips. It's one of those activities that's fun to do with the children and always evokes nostalgic childhood memories in the adults.

Here I've combined the flavours of s'mores in a cookie so that you can enjoy that campfire treat all year round.

MAKES AROUND 25 COOKIES

340g plain flour
1 tsp bicarbonate of soda
1 tsp salt
2 tsp ground cinnamon
230g butter
170g granulated sugar
130g soft brown sugar
2 tbsp honey
1 tsp vanilla extract
2 large eggs
250g chocolate chips
100g mini marshmallows

prep: 15 minutes, cook: 20 minutes

Preheat the oven to 180°C fan/200°C/gas mark 6 and line 2 baking sheets with greaseproof paper. In a small bowl combine the flour, bicarbonate of soda, salt and cinnamon and set aside.

In a large bowl, cream together the butter, both sugars, honey and the vanilla extract, then add the egg and mix well. Gradually add the flour mixture until well combined and then stir in the chocolate chips and mini marshmallows.

Spoon the dough onto the sheets, one tablespoon at a time, allowing space in between each cookie as the mixture will spread. Bake for about 9 minutes until the edges are cooked and browned and the middle is still gooey. Cool a little before transferring to a wire rack. Best served slightly warm.

CHUTNEY SAUSAGE ROLLS & CHOPPED SALAD

Sausage rolls conjure up memories of children's parties and picnics as well as a late-night feast having left work late or left the pub even later! Shop-bought pastries are OK, but homemade is top-notch and worth the effort. We're big fans of sausage rolls and Scotch eggs in our family and I usually make a batch of these sausage rolls at Christmas as a cheeky nibble with some cocktails. The girls love them for supper with a simple chopped salad which gets made weekly throughout the year.

The salad is just any vegetables that are in the fridge, all chopped up and seasoned with a little lemon juice and salt. No oil or anything else, as it doesn't need it. It's a great distraction activity for the girls. They have their own knives and chopping boards, and usually gather all that they need and get started without any prompting. I love watching them taste and season the salad. They've obviously watched me do it far too many times and act as if they're on a cookery show while preparing everything.

The sausage rolls can be made into bite-sized pieces or slightly bigger for a main meal. Serve them cold the following day with a chopped salad, some cheese, chutney and crackers for a quick ploughman's-style lunch.

275g plain flour

200g unsalted butter, cold and
cubed

200ml ice cold water (you may
not need all of the water)

½ tsp salt

1 egg to glaze

extra butter to grease

450g sausages or good quality
sausage meat

1 garlic clove, crushed or
minced

½-1 tsp chilli flakes

½ tbsp fennel seeds, lightly
toasted and ground

200g chutney – onion
marmalade or chilli and
tomato chutney

black and white sesame seeds
to decorate

prep: 40 minutes, cook: 20 minutes

To make the rough puff pastry put the flour and salt into a large bowl
and add the cold and cubed butter. Using a rounded-edge knife,
stir the butter into the flour so that it's coated in the flour. Add the
lemon juice and enough of the water to bind the dough, adding one
tablespoon at a time if that's easier. It shouldn't be a sticky or a wet
dough, but moist and lumpy from the cubes of butter.

Tip the dough out onto a lightly floured work surface and shape it
into a brick by gently patting and bringing the dough together with
lightly floured hands. Using a floured rolling pin, roll it out into a
long rectangle (about 45cm x 15cm) then fold it in 3 like a business
letter. Fold the bottom ⅓ up over the middle ⅓, then fold the top ⅓
down to cover them. Turn the dough and repeat the process of rolling
out and folding before wrapping it in cling-film and putting it in the
fridge to chill and rest for 15-30 minutes. Repeat the rolling out and
folding process 2-3 times and chill for a final 20 minutes before
using it.

While the pastry is resting, remove the skins from the sausages and
place them in a bowl. Add the crushed garlic clove, chilli flakes,
toasted fennel seeds, a little salt and pepper and mix well.

Roll out the pastry into 2 long rectangles, about 5 inches wide and
to the thickness of a pound coin. Divide the sausage meat in two and
roll into long sausages to fit the pastry, you may find this easier using
floured hands and a lightly floured work surface.

Spread the chutney onto the pastry, making sure not to spread it
right to the edges. Place the long sausages on top of the chutney.
Beat the egg with a pinch of salt and brush along one long edge of
the pastry then fold the other edge around the sausage and chutney
to seal. Use a fork to crimp the length of the sausage roll then trim
the ends.

Using the egg wash, glaze the sausage rolls then cut them into your
preferred size. 2½cm/1-inch sausage rolls are good as a snack/
canapé size, 10cm/4-inch rolls are good to have as an indulgent
lunch with a fresh salad. Once you've cut the sausage rolls, slash the
tops of them, place on a baking tray lined with greaseproof paper
and bake in a preheated oven set to 200°C fan/220°C/gas mark 7
for 15-18 minutes until golden brown. Leave to cool slightly as the
chutney will be piping hot. Best served warm.

For the chopped salad, roughly chop up a pepper, 1-2 tomatoes,
3 spring onions or ½ red onion, ½ avocado and a 4cm piece of
cucumber. Mix them together in a small bowl and season with a little
salt and a squeeze of lemon or lime juice. You can add some fresh
herbs like coriander too if you have some to hand. Simple and tasty
with lots of crunch.

POTATO, ROSEMARY & BLUE CHEESE LOAF

In 1942, the Federation of Bakers was established and created the National Loaf; a dense and grey loaf using wheatmeal or wholemeal flour. Imported white flour was in short supply, and so, to utilise home-grown wheat, the National Loaf was created, making use of every part of the crop – grain and chaff. It was eaten by everyone, even the royal family, although not many liked it. Another way of stretching any available white flour was to create a loaf using potatoes. In the interest of palatability and flavour, herbs were added to the dough before baking.

MAKES 1 LOAF

300g potatoes, peeled and chopped (about 380g unpeeled weight)

300g white spelt flour

1 tsp dried-active yeast

1 tsp salt

1 tsp caster sugar

1 tbsp chopped fresh rosemary

4-5 sprigs fresh rosemary

3-4 tbsp olive oil, plus extra for kneading

10 baby new potatoes

150g Gorgonzola cheese

sea salt, to taste

prep: 40 minutes, cook: 30 minutes

Bring the potatoes to the boil in a large pan of water then simmer for 15 minutes, or until tender. Drain them in a colander over a bowl to reserve the cooking liquid. Measure 130ml of the liquid and put to one side. Place the potatoes back in the hot saucepan for a few minutes to dry out.

Place the flour, yeast, salt, sugar and the chopped rosemary in a large bowl and mix until evenly distributed. Mash the potatoes with the olive oil, add to the flour mixture and mix well.

Add the reserved potato water gradually. Once the mixture is well combined and has come together into a ball, tip out onto a clean work surface and use a little olive oil to help with the kneading. Knead for about 10 minutes, or until the dough feels smooth. Place into a lightly oiled bowl, cover with oiled cling film and leave to prove in a warm place for at least an hour.

Clean and halve the new potatoes and parboil in salted water. Keep to one side until needed for the topping.

Preheat the oven to 200°C fan/220°C/gas mark 7 and generously grease a 2lb loaf tin. Tip the dough out onto a lightly floured surface and form it into a rectangle, the same size as the loaf tin. Cover and leave to prove for 30 minutes.

Chop the cooled boiled potatoes into quarters and scatter them over the top of the loaf along with the crumbled Gorgonzola. Drizzle some olive oil on top and finish with the sprigs of rosemary and a sprinkle of sea salt. Bake for 30 minutes until golden brown.

RAINY DAY FAIRY CAKES

My parents worked away a lot when I was young. Neither of them was in the forces, they worked in television and would travel the world filming different programmes, meaning that either Mam-gu or Nan and Dups would be drafted in to babysit me and my brother Gareth. It was during these stints that I would learn different recipes from Mam-gu and Nan, and it was my favourite thing in the world to do – standing next to one of them in the kitchen, getting as close as I could and watching every move of what we were making or baking. Activities ranged from baking cakes, breads, pies, pasties and biscuits to making supper for us all to eat later that day. We would also play board games, cards and my favourite: boy, girl, fish, fruit …

I feel so fortunate to have been able to spend that time with my grandmothers. It's how we bonded, over a love of food and cooking and just really enjoying each other's company, regardless of the age gap. I miss Mam-gu every day, and wish she could have met Mari and Alys, but I know she's with us in some shape or form. Being able to spend time with Nan, and the girls getting to know her is truly precious. When I watch her playing with them, it takes me back to being their age and me doing the exact same thing with Nan.

MAKES 12 FAIRY CAKES

165g butter, soft

165g light-brown sugar

3 large eggs

175g self-raising flour

15g cocoa powder

75g dark chocolate

ICING

150g soft, unsalted butter

120g icing sugar

30g cocoa powder

2 tbsp milk

hundreds and thousands to decorate

prep: 20 minutes, cook: 20 minutes

Preheat the oven to 160°C fan/180°C/gas mark 4 and line a 12-hole muffin tin with 12 cupcake cases.

Place the butter, sugar and eggs into a large mixing bowl and sieve the flour and cocoa powder on top. Mix with an electric hand mixer until smooth. Melt the chocolate in a bowl over a pan of hot water or in a microwave oven for 20 second bursts. Pour the melted chocolate into the cupcake batter and stir to combine.

Divide the mixture between the cupcake cases and bake in the middle of the oven for 18 minutes. Check that they're cooked by inserting a cocktail stick which should come out clean if they're ready. Leave to cool in the tin for 5-10 minutes, then remove to cool completely on a wire rack.

To make the buttercream, sieve the icing sugar and cocoa powder into a medium bowl, add the soft butter and cream them together until smooth, adding in the milk a tablespoon at a time.

Decorate the cupcakes with the buttercream either by using a piping bag or by spreading the mixture on top of each cake with a palette knife.

Sprinkle the hundreds and thousands on top and try to resist eating them all at once.

CHAPTER 5

SOLO SUPPERS

In 2016, my husband started working away while the girls and I settled into our new house back in my hometown of Cardiff. I couldn't wait to be near my parents and Nan again. Having my school friends nearby too would be a great support and present endless opportunities to meet and catch up.

In reality this didn't happen. I put so much energy into ensuring that the girls settled into their new school and nursery, making sure that they made friends in class and continued with their after-school activities, that I didn't make enough time for myself. While the girls adjusted and settled amazingly, I, on the other hand, didn't.

There was a certain sense of unease. I wouldn't call it loneliness. How could I be lonely, surrounded by loving friends and family? So why couldn't I settle? Was it the house move? Settling the girls in their new surroundings? Being away from Matt? Then it came to me.

One evening while I was sitting on the sofa having just put the girls to bed and wondering what to eat for supper, I realised that my diet had become lazy. What's more, I wasn't exercising as much and wasn't really taking proper care of myself.

That lightbulb moment not only got me off the sofa to cook myself something delicious, it made me think about others who might have fallen into the same rut as me – not just military wives and partners, but anyone who, for whatever reason, is cooking for one. It also spurred me to talk about it and share ideas for solo suppers on social media, and I'm pleased to say that many have felt inspired to cook properly for themselves after seeing my posts.

The suppers are often based on leftovers and whatever is in the fridge, freezer and cupboard. Here are some of my absolute favourites that can be made easily for one or more should you have company joining you for supper.

CHICKEN, NOODLE & VEGETABLE COCONUT BROTH

This is my go-to solo supper and the perfect meal for one to enjoy and slurp noisily. The recipe makes enough for two portions so I usually freeze half of it to enjoy another time. There are quite a few ingredients, but don't let that put you off as it's relatively quick to make. The paste is fresh and worth making extra so that you can freeze it to add to stir-fries.

I often change what I have in the broth too, depending on my mood and what's in the fridge or freezer. It's delicious with prawns or just with vegetables. I sometimes serve it with rice instead of noodles too. The essence of the dish is the broth so it's up to you what you have in it.

SERVES 2

1 small onion

2 tsp oil

1 tsp each of garam masala, ground cumin, ground coriander and turmeric

3-4 garlic cloves

½ fresh chilli, red or green

4cm piece of ginger

200ml chicken stock

200ml coconut milk

2-3 chicken thighs

½ sweet potato

3 mushrooms, chestnut or portobello

handful of fine green beans

handful of greens (pak choi/ spinach/cabbage)

small handful of coriander

salt and pepper to taste

250g noodles

TO SERVE

½ fresh chilli

coriander leaves

lime

chopped peanuts or cashew nuts

a spring onion

crispy onions – usually near the condiments in the supermarket

prep: 20 minutes, cook: 20 minutes

Start by making the paste. Pop the onion, garlic, ginger, chilli, coriander stalks, a glug of oil and a good pinch of salt in a food processor and blitz until you have a paste.

Prepare all the other ingredients before you start to cook as the dish doesn't take long to prepare. Wash, peel and chop the sweet potato into 2cm cubes and roast them in a preheated oven set to 200°C fan/220°C/gas mark 7 for 15-20 minutes. Wash and chop the green beans into thirds, wash and shred the greens, wipe and slice the mushrooms and roughly chop the chicken thighs

In a medium saucepan over a medium heat, fry the paste in a little oil for a couple of minutes before adding the spices followed by the coconut milk and stock. Bring to the boil then reduce to a simmer. Add the chicken and cook for about 4-5 minutes before adding the green beans. After a couple of minutes add the mushrooms and the greens. Once the sweet potato has roasted and has taken on some colour, add to the broth for a couple of minutes.

Prepare all the garnishes at this point – slice the chilli and spring onion thinly, finely chop the nuts, wash the coriander and slice the lime.

Cook the noodles according to the packet instructions. The broth is ready when the chicken is cooked – check a small piece to make sure you're happy. Taste to check the seasoning, adding salt or a crack of black pepper.

Serve the noodles in a large bowl and then ladle on the chicken and vegetable broth. Garnish with coriander, spring onion, chilli, chopped nuts, crispy onions and a squeeze of lime – and I recommend tucking a napkin into your top to prevent any splashes of broth.

It's a great bowl of food and
never fails to fill me with
warmth and goodness.

SAUSAGE & LENTIL ONE POT

This dish is a one-pot wonder to cook and only requires one bowl and one spoon to eat. This warmer goes well on a cold, dark winter's night while you're curled up on the sofa, under a blanket watching your favourite film. The recipe can easily be adapted by adding more vegetables and swapping sausages for cod, which is slightly lighter but just as delicious. The cod and lentils are one of Dad's favourites and I'll sometimes make it just for the two of us when Mam's out on the razzle.

The recipe makes enough for three meals, and so I tend to freeze two portions for a later date. What I like most about this dish is that I usually have the ingredients in the house, and so if I'm tired I can switch off my brain and go into autopilot mode to make it. While the pan is simmering and cooking the lentils I put the girls to bed and then enjoy the hot steaming stew in my favourite bowl with my favourite wooden spoon.

SERVES 3

1 tbsp olive oil

2 rashers streaky smoked bacon

6 sausages – either pork, Cumberland, Lincolnshire – whatever you fancy

1 large onion

1 large carrot

2 celery sticks

5 garlic cloves

2 tbsp tomato purée

1 tsp dried thyme

a good pinch of dried chilli flakes

250g green or puy lentils

600ml chicken or vegetable stock

a little fresh parsley to serve (optional)

salt and pepper to taste

serve with green beans or broccoli

prep: 15 minutes, cook: 50 minutes

Start by getting everything roughly chopped, including the bacon, onion, carrot, celery and garlic. Place the oil in a medium pan on a medium to high heat and add the sausages. Brown them on all sides, turning frequently. Reduce the heat and add the bacon for a minute before adding the onion, carrot and celery. Stir to coat the vegetables in the oil and cover for about 5 minutes so that the vegetables sweat and soften – stir occasionally.

Next add the garlic and cook for a couple of minutes. Add the tomato purée, dried thyme and chilli flakes and give everything a good stir. Add the lentils and stock and stir to combine. Bring up to the boil and then reduce to a simmer, putting the lid on, but leaving it slightly ajar. Cook the lentils for about 40 minutes until soft and tender. Check the seasoning, adding salt and pepper if required. Serve with your choice of greens.

VEGETABLE & PASTA SOUP

As solo suppers go, this is always in my back pocket as one that I can easily throw together if I'm tired but in need of something tasty and comforting. Soup is definitely in my top five favourite foods to make and eat. I could easily write a whole book on soups, from single vegetable variations to more complex and full flavoured pots. Soup is something that you can make from next to nothing – just some stock and vegetables, cooked up and blitzed. What could be easier?

I always have some stock cubes and dried pasta in the cupboard, then I just raid the fridge and freezer for whatever vegetables I can find. At the end, I sometimes add pesto, a grating of Parmesan cheese or just a little drizzle of olive oil, plenty of pepper and a sprinkle of chilli flakes.

If you really can't be bothered to do anything too fancy, then some stock, a handful of pasta and peas from the freezer with a grating of Parmesan cheese is just the right amount of everything that you need to make this soup in its simplest form.

SERVES 1

1 chicken or vegetable stock cube

a handful of small pasta

1 medium carrot

a handful of peas

¼ courgette

a handful of broccoli

Parmesan cheese or pesto to finish

prep: 5 minutes, cook: 10 minutes

Peel and finely chop the carrot and finely chop the courgette. Put them in a small saucepan along with the stock cube and 500ml of water and bring to the boil. Reduce to a simmer and add the pasta; as the pasta is small it shouldn't take more than 5-7 minutes to cook. Add the peas for the last 2 minutes, check the seasoning and serve in a giant bowl. Grate Parmesan cheese on the surface or add a spoonful of pesto. Alternatively, add a drizzle of olive oil, some black pepper and a sprinkle of chilli flakes.

KEDGEREE FOR ONE

This may seem like a rather indulgent supper, but when you look down the list of ingredients there's nothing really that fancy, it's just a good, honest, tasty meal that doesn't take long to make. To me, it's one of the best comfort foods you can cook, which is why I make it often to enjoy by myself after a long, busy day.

Traditionally kedgeree would be served for breakfast and was a firm favourite on the breakfast menus at many an officers' mess. It was believed to have been brought to the UK by British colonials who had eaten and enjoyed the dish during the Victorian era. It's also believed to be something that the Scottish Regiments created when they started to miss the tastes of India. Although the recipe below is for one person, you can easily double the quantities to feed two or increase to feed more. I often throw in a large handful of peas or some frozen spinach at the end of the rice cooking just to add a bit of colour and some veg, but in its purest form it's simply delicious.

SERVES 1-2

a knob of butter

½ tbsp oil

¼ onion, finely chopped

2 cardamom pods, slightly bashed

¼ tsp turmeric

¼ tsp ground cinnamon

1 bay leaf

75g basmati rice

180ml fish, vegetable or chicken stock

freshly ground black pepper

125g naturally smoked haddock fillet

1 medium egg

a couple of parsley sprigs, roughly chopped

a wedge of lemon

prep: 20 minutes, cook: 20 minutes

Heat the butter and oil in a medium saucepan, add the finely chopped onion and cook gently over a medium heat until soft. Add the bashed cardamom pods, turmeric, cinnamon and bay leaf, then cook for a further minute. Pour in the rice and stir until it's well coated in the spices and onions. Pour in the stock, add a good pinch of salt and some black pepper and bring to the boil. Stir the mixture and cover with a lid, then reduce the heat and leave to cook gently for 12 minutes.

While the rice cooks, bring some water to the boil in a small pan, add the haddock and simmer for 4 minutes, until it's just cooked. Remove the fish carefully and leave to cool enough to handle. Flake the fish, making sure to discard any bones and skin. Boil the egg for 6-7 minutes. Drain and peel and keep to one side. Remove the bay leaves from the rice, then gently fluff it with a fork. Add the fish, cover again and heat for a further 2 minutes. Heap the rice and fish onto a plate. Chop the egg into quarters and add to the plate and sprinkle over the chopped parsley. Serve with a wedge of lemon.

APPLE & OAT PANCAKES

I have to admit that I used to make this after everyone in our house had eaten their breakfast because I didn't want to share it with anyone else! There's not much sugar in the pancakes as I don't have a sweet tooth, but I find that the fruit is enough to sweeten them.

The oats in this recipe are a good alternative to flour and make a great breakfast or brunch dish. I often use leftover apple sauce from Sunday lunch in this recipe, but you can easily make the stewed apple.

MAKES 6-8 10CM/4-INCH PANCAKES

160g oats

1 eating apple

1 egg

1½ tsp baking powder

½ tsp cinnamon or apple pie spice blend

1 tbsp honey

250ml milk

vegetable oil to grease

TO SERVE

150g mixed berries

1 tbsp honey

Greek yoghurt

prep: 20 minutes, cook: 20 minutes

Peel, core and chop the apple and place it in a small saucepan on a medium heat with a drop of water. Cook for a few minutes until soft and you're able to mash the apple with a fork. Alternatively, you can purée the apple using a blender, then leave to cook.

In a food processor, blitz 120g of the oats until they resemble flour, then add to a mixing bowl along with the remaining 40g of whole oats. Add the cooled puréed apple, honey, baking powder, cinnamon, egg and milk and mix into a relatively thick batter.

Place a small frying pan over a medium heat and grease with a little oil – use a piece of kitchen towel to wipe away any excess. Spoon the mixture into the pan until the pancake is roughly 10cm in diameter. Turn the heat down to a low-medium setting as the pancakes can colour quickly. Cook them for about 2 minutes or until golden then flip using a palette knife or spatula. Cook for a further minute then serve.

While cooking the pancakes, quickly make some stewed fruit by placing the berries along with the honey and a drop of water in a small saucepan and cook for a few minutes over a medium heat until some of the fruit have broken down to create a delicious compote. Keep warm until ready to serve.

When you're ready to serve, place 2-3 pancakes on a plate with a good spoonful of yoghurt and a good amount of the compote.

TACOS FOR ONE

I love Mexican food. It's full of flavour, vibrant and sociable – it's a real crowd pleaser, but that doesn't stop me from having one of my favourite cuisines as a solo supper. It's one of those dishes that doesn't take long to prepare, but I feel like I'm treating myself when I make this feast. I'm a huge fan of refried beans, but the stuff you can get in tins in the UK is just awful and so I started making my own in order to satisfy my addiction.

If my husband was home, this dish would probably need to include meat, and so that's another reason why I happily make it for myself to enjoy – I don't have to share it with anyone. The beans now make a regular appearance when we have fajitas together as a family, and both my daughters love them as much as I do … so does my husband, just as long as there's some chicken or pork there too.

I've never been to Mexico, but have eaten some authentic dishes in restaurants in London as well as on family holidays to California, but I hope to make the trip there one day in order to fully immerse myself in the culture and cuisine … for now, I will continue to enjoy my solo taco sessions and dream of Mexico.

SERVES 1

1 tbsp oil

1 tin black beans

1 small onion, roughly chopped

2 garlic cloves, grated

a good pinch of chilli flakes

½ tsp each ground cumin,
coriander, smoked paprika
and oregano

salt to season

¼ avocado

handful or cherry tomatoes

small bunch of fresh coriander

juice of ½ lime

2 spring onions

handful of lettuce leaves

30g feta or grated Cheddar
cheese

4-5 soft tacos

prep: 20 minutes, cook: 15 minutes

For the beans, heat the oil in a small saucepan and sweat the onion, garlic and chilli flakes for a couple of minutes. Add the spices after 5 minutes and cook for a further minute while stirring. Meanwhile, drain the black beans, but keep the water from the can then blitz the beans in a food processor or mash with a masher/fork then add to the pan. Mix everything together and reduce the heat. Add the reserved bean water if this mixture gets too thick – but don't let it become too liquid.

Chop the avocado and tomatoes into 1cm cubes and pop into a small bowl. Roughly chop the coriander and add to the avocado along with a squeeze of lime and some salt. You can add some chopped fresh chilli too. Wash and shred the lettuce and place in a bowl and either crumble the feta or grate the Cheddar cheese into another bowl and finally slice the spring onions and add to yet another little bowl.

Just before you're ready to serve, warm the soft tacos in a pan or in a microwave for a few seconds then it's time to eat. I usually serve everything on a wooden tray for me to enjoy by myself in front of the TV. I only eat half of the beans and freeze the other half to have on another day with some rice and a salad or for another solo taco session at another time.

Assemble the tacos as you like – I usually dollop on some beans and then add some lettuce, the avocado and tomato salsa, spring onions and then a little cheese to finish. Delicious. All you need now is a margarita!

EGG BANJO

I know the name of this recipe might cause confusion, but the banjo is, in fact, a fried egg sandwich, named because of the comical reaction of the eater to a runny egg yolk dribbling down their clothing. When the egg starts oozing out, the sandwich is quickly raised out of harm's way in one hand while the other hand roughly 'strums' the shirt-front area in a vain attempt to prevent staining. If you're trying this now – you're playing the egg banjo!

My darling husband introduced me to them, even though I'd been enjoying fried egg sandwiches in blissful ignorance since I was eight years old, but had no idea I'd actually been eating egg banjos until he enlightened me.

As sandwiches go, the fried egg variety has to be one of the best ones around. It's an army breakfast staple as well as a civvy street favourite, and one that's easy to make when you need something quick, tasty and filling.

When my husband was serving with the Grenadier Guards, they would be up very early getting ready for Trooping the Colour – and when I say early, I mean up at the crack of dawn. After rehearsing, they'd all go back to the barracks to get ready for the main parade and wolf down an egg banjo, trying very hard not to get any yolk or sauce down their glorious red tunics ahead of going back out to the main troop … what an image!

My nan makes the best egg banjos of course, and as a student I'd call her up and see if I could have one for breakfast – they will sort out any hangover. I'm not sure if it was the fact that Nan was making me breakfast or the combination of a hot fried egg on buttered white bread with ketchup dripping out of the bottom, but those fried egg sandwiches were amazing. I still love going over to Nan's to have breakfast, a cuppa and a chat with her.

Now, of course, you can buy and enjoy whatever bread you want, but I've included a simple bread roll or bap recipe which will help make a great egg banjo.

SERVES 4-6

250g strong white bread flour

5g salt

5g fast acting yeast

30g butter, soft

100ml water

60ml milk

1-2 eggs per person

olive oil

salt and pepper

any condiment of your choice

prep: 30 minutes, cook: 30 minutes

Place the flour, salt and yeast into a medium bowl and stir to combine. Rub in the butter then add the water and milk and bring the mixture together to form a ball of dough. Tip it onto a clean work surface and knead until smooth. This will take 5-8 minutes. Don't be tempted to add any flour. It's the kneading that will make the dough smooth and elastic, not any added flour.

Once the dough feels smooth and bounces back when poked, place it back into the bowl, cover with a tea towel and leave for 1-2 hours or until it has doubled in size. There's no need to put it in a warm place, just somewhere it can rest and prove.

After proving, divide the dough into 4-6 pieces, depending on the size of bap you're after. Shape the pieces one by one into round balls and leave to prove for a second time on a baking tray lined with greaseproof paper and cover them with a tea towel again. Leave to prove for about 35-45 minutes.

Preheat the oven to 180°C fan/200°C/gas mark 7. Bake the baps for roughly 20 minutes until golden brown, then leave to cool completely.

The tricky part is frying the eggs. Place a tablespoon of oil in a medium frying pan over a medium-high heat. Crack 1-2 eggs per banjo into the pan and leave until they start to crisp on the edges before carefully flipping them over. Cook the eggs to your preferred consistency.

Meanwhile, slice open the baps and butter generously. Place 1-2 eggs in each bap and serve with plenty of sauce and lots of kitchen roll. Oh, and try not to get any yolk or sauce down your top please!

CHOCOLATE BREAD

When I was seventeen, Emily, one of my best friends, used to work in a 24-hour supermarket, and during her break on the night shift I would often drive over to see her and we would have a car park picnic. Now this picnic wasn't anything fancy, no cutlery was used, or serviettes deployed, and the car was always in a state afterwards – much worse than usual. We usually bought the same items to graze on: cheese and chive dip was a favourite with crisps and carrots sticks, a selection from the deli counter including chicken satay skewers and samosas and then pudding – well, this was the best bit and the one we looked forward to the most – a freshly baked loaf of chocolate bread from the bakery.

I'm not ashamed to say that we tore through that loaf at an impressive rate of knots at every car park picnic sitting, and it had nothing to do with the amount of time Emily had for her break. That loaf was everything that you could ever wish for – delicious little morsels of chocolate chips evenly distributed throughout the bread and the dough itself wasn't overly sweet, but perfectly balanced against the chocolate and slightly buttery in flavour – like a cheat's brioche. We would have the best catch-ups during our picnics and looking back, those night shifts served as a practice run for Emily who's now a paedriatric A&E sister in Cardiff.

I've tried my very best to recreate the loaf of bread here for you to try – perfect for a picnic lunch or at any time of the day, just be warned that it won't last long!

MAKES 1 LOAF

500g strong white flour

250ml full fat milk, warm

15g yeast

10g salt

100g butter

60g caster sugar

1 egg

1 egg for glaze

200g good quality dark chocolate chips

prep: 30 minutes, cook: 30 minutes

To make the dough, place the flour, salt and yeast in a large mixing bowl and rub in the butter. Add the sugar and mix until evenly distributed. Add the egg and milk and mix until a ball of dough forms, then tip it out onto a work surface. Knead the dough for 8-10 minutes until it's smooth and elastic. Put it back into the bowl and leave to prove for about an hour until double in size.

Once proved, knock the dough back and knead in the chocolate chips. Once they're evenly distributed, you can either shape the dough and place it in a greased 2lb loaf tin or shape it into a tight ball and place on a greased baking tray. Whichever one you choose, cover the dough with a tea towel and leave for 45 minutes to rise again.

Preheat the oven to 180°C fan/200°C/gas mark 6. Uncover the risen dough and gently brush it with a beaten egg, slash the top of the loaf with a sharp knife and bake on the middle shelf of the oven for 25-30 minutes.

Once baked, leave to cool completely before cutting a huge chunk to devour.

AUNTY 'RENE'S BANANA BREAD

You may think it a bit bizarre that I've included a cake recipe in my Solo Suppers chapter, especially in light of the fact that I don't have a sweet tooth. However, this particular recipe reminds me of going to a little café just down the road from my parents' house when I was young, and I would always order the banana bread as my cake of choice, while others would go for a wedge of chocolate cake. It's an understated cake that doesn't need to shout or be highly decorated to get attention. What's more, it's so easy to make and tasty too, plus it makes good use of those odd bananas that are often left in the bowl.

I'm a big fan of bananas. They make the best grab-and-go snack, or mid-morning/afternoon pick me up. Slice them into porridge or a smoothie to add sweetness and substance, or top on toast with almond butter – my favourite pre-race breakfast of choice. Slice and freeze them to make a simple banana ice cream; mash them and make a pancake batter or save the overripe fruit from the compost bin and transform them into a delicious cake.

This recipe is a no-frills version from my great aunty Irene. I often ad-lib and throw in any number of extra ingredients, like chocolate chips, nuts, dried fruit, caramel pieces – whatever you fancy. I include it as a solo supper recipe, even though it might be eaten mid-afternoon when you're working from home and have set yourself a 3:30pm deadline before stopping to make a cuppa and slice a piece of banana bread.

My guilty secret is that I spread some butter on top too, just for added decadence.

MAKES 1 LARGE LOAF

215g plain flour

2 tsp baking powder

¼ tsp bicarbonate of soda

½ tsp salt

60g butter, melted

2 eggs

100g caster sugar

100g light-brown sugar

1 tsp vanilla extract

2 medium ripe bananas, mashed

prep: 15 minutes, cook: 1 hour

Preheat the oven to 160°C fan/180°C/gas mark 4. Grease and line a 900g/2lb loaf tin and set to one side.

Sieve the flour, baking powder and bicarbonate of soda into a medium mixing bowl and add the salt and sugar, giving everything a good stir.

In a separate bowl, mix together the melted butter, egg and vanilla and add to the dry ingredients, stirring until everything has just combined. Fold in the mashed bananas and pour the mixture into the prepared tin. Bake in the middle of the oven for 50-55 minutes. Leave to cool before slicing and eating. The loaf will keep for 3-5 days in an airtight box and freezes very well.

WELSH RAREBIT

This is the first recipe I remember making on my own after school when I was a little girl – which I guess makes it my first ever solo supper. It's a recipe that I still love due to its ease to make when I fancy something quick and tasty. The ingredients are simple and always to hand – the mix of mature Cheddar, cheese, Dijon mustard and Worcestershire sauce delivers a good hit of flavour without being too complicated.

I sometimes add some sautéed leek or finely chopped red onion. Fried, chopped, smoked bacon is another good addition.

SERVES 1

2 slices of your favourite bread

125g of cheese, preferably
    mature

1 large egg

1 heaped tsp Dijon mustard

a good shake of Worcestershire
    sauce

salt and pepper to taste

prep: 10 minutes, cook: 10 minutes

Grate the Cheddar cheese into a bowl and add the egg, Dijon mustard and Worcestershire sauce and mix well. Add a pinch of salt and pepper and any extra ingredients and stir to combine.

Grill the bread on one side. Turn the slices over, divide the mixture between them and spread evenly before popping back under the grill to cook and colour. This won't take long, just a couple of minutes, which is enough time for you to grab a plate and cutlery.

The next time you fancy cheese on toast, try this instead – I can guarantee you won't go back!

HARICOT BEANS & VEGETABLE GRATIN

Nan always tells me that if I have a number of tinned items in my cupboard I can always make something to eat. Tinned beans and pulses as well as dried lentils and tinned tomatoes with some vegetables can be made into a multitude of dishes. While researching recipes in the Imperial War Museum, I found a recipe for haricot beans au gratin in a 1947 Ministry of Food leaflet. It sounded simple to make using a handful of ingredients from the store cupboard. I imagine that the dish would have been a tasty light lunch.

The idea behind the leaflets issued by the Ministry of Food was to inspire households to cook different dishes using items that they may already have in the cupboard or to try new dishes. I happily sat reading my way through many such leaflets, numerous menu cards and recipes, absorbing all the information and wondering what my grandmothers would have been cooking during the Second World War and afterwards.

This simple recipe inspired me to make a solo supper that is rather decadent, which is why I don't make it very often, but once in a while I do fancy something that's rich, creamy and indulgent, so this dish fits the brief and is quick to make. If you don't have smoked bacon then leave it out but it's worth making the effort with the topping of breadcrumbs and hazelnuts, as this gives much needed texture to the dish.

SERVES 2

½ tbsp olive oil

3 rashers of smoked streaky bacon

1 small onion

1 small carrot

handful of runner/French beans

¼ Savoy cabbage, shredded thinly

1 garlic clove

1 bay leaf

3 cloves

1 tin haricot beans, drained

salt and freshly grated nutmeg to season

200ml double cream

1 slice of bread, blitzed into breadcrumbs

40g Parmesan cheese

10g hazelnuts, roughly chopped

prep: 20 minutes, cook: 20 minutes

Roughly chop the onion and carrot to about the same size as the haricot beans, cut the green beans into 2cm pieces and finely shred the cabbage. Heat the oil in a medium pan and gently cook the onion and carrot until soft, using the lid to trap the steam which will cook the vegetables more quickly. Roughly chop and add the bacon, then give everything a good stir and cook for about 5 minutes.

Then add the green beans, cabbage, garlic, bay leaf and cloves and continue to cook for about 2-3 minutes with the lid on. Add the haricot beans and the cream and turn the heat down low. Add 30g of the Parmesan cheese, stir and taste, before seasoning with the salt and nutmeg. Meanwhile, heat the grill to high.

Transfer the beans and vegetables to an oven proof dish and sprinkle the breadcrumbs, the remaining Parmesan cheese and the chopped hazelnuts on top and brown under the preheated grill until golden, bubbling and almost charred.

Serve from the grill with some crusty bread and a glass of crisp dry white wine.

MY MARMALADE

During the Second World War, Seville oranges, used to make marmalade, were difficult to get hold of. Other fruits and even vegetables were therefore used to make the British breakfast spread, with grated carrots and parsnips often used as a substitute.

Here's my no-frills marmalade which I make in January when Seville oranges are available in the shops. I usually make double the quantity stated below. I call it no-frills as I tend to throw the peel into a food processor to do the chopping for me, but by all means feel free to slice the peel into beautiful thin slithers if you want to.

Breakfast is an important meal and I love nothing more than sitting down to devour some toasted sourdough, unsalted butter and a jar of homemade marmalade. Ideally I'd be on my own to enjoy breakfast in peace and quiet, but that doesn't happen often.

I've been told that my marmalade has healing properties and is especially good for hangovers – any excuse to eat it if you ask me!

**FILLS APPROX.
12 X 450G/1LB JARS**

1kg Seville oranges

1kg granulated sugar

1kg Demerara sugar

juice of 1 lemon

2½ litres cold water

HOW TO STERILISE JARS

To make sure the jars are clean and sterile; firstly wash them with their lids in hot soapy water, then rinse but don't dry them with a towel. Place them on a baking tray in the oven, preheated to about 140°C fan/160°C/gas mark 3 and leave them to dry out. This usually takes about 10 minutes. Soak the lids in boiling water for a few minutes. Once dry, be careful not to touch the inside of the jars and once the marmalade is ready, carefully pour or ladle it into the jars. Seal with the lids and leave to cool. The heat will seal the jars and cause suction so that when the jar is opened you should hear a popping sound.

prep: 1 hour, cook: 2½-3 hours

On day 1, have a large bowl and a food processor ready. Remove the knobbly bit at the top of the oranges and give them a good wash to get rid of any dirt. Cut the oranges in half and squeeze the juice into the bowl then tear or cut the skin into 2-3 pieces and pop into the food processor, pips, pith and all. Whizz the oranges in batches and to your desired size of 'bits', then add to the juice in the bowl. Once you've done this with all the oranges, add the cold water and give it a good stir. Cover the bowl loosely with some cling film or foil and leave the mixture to mingle for 8-10 hours or overnight.

Next, transfer the mixture to a large pan, making sure that you have enough space to add the sugars as well as space for the mixture to swell slightly and boil. There's nothing worse than cleaning a hob covered in burnt-on marmalade – that would be me trying to be clever and not using a big enough pan!

Bring the mixture to the boil and then reduce to a simmer and leave for 1½ hours, stirring occasionally. After this time, turn the heat up to medium and add the sugars, stirring until dissolved. Then turn the heat up to the boil. Leave to boil for 25-35 minutes and do not stir. Pop a couple of plates into the freezer to be used to test if the marmalade has set. You'll notice that a lot of the pips will have floated to the surface during this rolling boil, so scoop them out and discard them.

After boiling, spoon a little of the mixture onto one of the frozen plates and leave for about 15 seconds then drag a finger through it. If it holds its shape then the marmalade is set, but if the mixture runs back together then boil it for a further 5 minutes before testing again. Once the marmalade is set, turn the heat off and leave it to settle for about 10-15 minutes, giving you a chance to get the jars ready.

Another method of sterilising is to wash and rinse the jars and lids, then pop them in the dishwasher on their own on a hot cycle. Once finished, fill with marmalade, as above.

Use a jug or a ladle to fill the jars with the hot marmalade, being careful not to burn your fingers. Seal the jars with their lids and leave out of reach and out of the way until they've cooled completely. Once cool, label the jars or quickly make yourself a round (or two) of hot buttered toast and slather on the scrumptious amber marmalade.

Store somewhere cool away from direct sunlight and the marmalade should keep for 2 years … not that it ever stays unopened for that long. Once opened, keep in the fridge and eat within 2 months.

CHAPTER 6

POSTINGS ABROAD

One benefit of being married into the armed forces family is the opportunity to travel and see the world. This may be the result of being posted somewhere for a couple of years, or due to operational tours or because of an exercise taking place anywhere that's not Brecon or Salisbury Plain. As a family, we've always been UK-based, but Matt has been fortunate to get to travel throughout his career and has been lucky enough to experience countries that many civilians won't ever get the chance to visit.

I sometimes hear stories of postings from some of my dear friends who are military wives. I always enjoy hearing about how you adapt and adjust to life when you're on the other side of the world, away from your family, trying to get settled in and carry on as normal. I take my hat off to all those who have done this and although I can't imagine how tough it must be to look after the family and sort them all out when you're in a different country, I hear nothing but fond memories of their adventures away from home, and the communities that rally around to make them feel at home.

In this chapter I've included a varied selection of recipes from across the globe that will hopefully inspire you to try something new.

OFFICERS' WIVES' DIP

The story goes that if you were an officer's wife and posted to Germany, there would be a social gathering of the wives on the patch to welcome new arrivals – the patch being the housing estate where the families are based. Someone in the group would whip up a batch of dip as a welcome offering and pass the recipe onto the new arrival in order for them to do the same for the next newbie wife. We've never been posted to Germany, and as a Senior Non-Commissioned Officer's wife, I would have missed out on this tradition – and so here is the recipe for us all to try.

I'm not sure if this is the definitive recipe as I've had several versions passed down to me. I love the story and tradition behind the recipe; being welcomed into the patch by lovely neighbours and like-minded females who have been in your shoes several times before.

A posting can be daunting, and food has that magical capability of bringing people together and breaking the ice to form new, lifelong friendships.

SERVES MANY!

2 tins of artichokes

450g of mayonnaise

180g of grated Parmesan cheese

2 garlic cloves

paprika

baguette for dipping

prep: 5 minutes, cook: 30 minutes

Place all the ingredients except the paprika into a food processor and blitz to combine. Scrape the mixture into an ovenproof dish, sprinkle a little paprika over the top and bake in the oven for 30 minutes. Serve with some crusty baguette, cut into cubes – it's not a dainty dip, but it sure is delicious.

WATERMELON SALAD

I want to include a watermelon recipe somewhere but I'm not sure where it belongs. When my husband was first deployed to Afghanistan, he bought some watermelon from a vendor on the side of the road which apparently was the best watermelon he has ever tasted – something he reminds me of every time we have watermelon. I daren't burst his bubble and say that it probably tasted amazing due to being thirst-quenching in the extremely hot climate, but instead I've decided to create a cooling recipe that is perfect to enjoy on a hot summer's day.

It's funny that a single ingredient can transport us to an exact moment in time, but it's also amazing that our senses evoke those memories so vividly to us. I know that the watermelon I buy now isn't quite the same as the one my husband had in Afghanistan, but that's not important – it's the memory that comes straight back to him and takes him back in time to that refreshing moment enjoying a break from his duties that day.

SERVES 4

500g watermelon

²⁄₃ cucumber

1 red onion

175g feta cheese

small bunch of mint

small bunch of parsley

extra virgin olive oil

juice of 1 lemon

1 large pitta bread

prep: 20 minutes: cook: 5 minutes

Chop the watermelon into bite-sized chunks and place into a large serving bowl. Cut the cucumber in half, lengthways and scoop out the seeds then cut into semi circles and add to the bowl. Cut the red onion in half, slice thinly, chop the feta cheese into chunks and add both to the bowl.

Roughly chop the mint and parsley and sprinkle over. Add a squeeze of lemon, drizzle some oil and sprinkle in a little salt before giving everything a good mix. Taste to check the seasoning. Toast the pitta bread and cut roughly into 2cm squares and stir into the salad just before serving.

This is a simple recipe that's an ideal side dish to accompany grilled meat or fish, best enjoyed in the heat of the summer sun so that it can cool and refresh you.

CHAO FAN – FRIED RICE

How do I describe Vicki, my military wife best friend? She's kind, thoughtful, stubborn, strong-willed, hilarious, straight-talking and wonderful. We met one evening at an Aldershot Military Wives Choir practice. She had just been posted to the area from Catterick. We found out that our husbands would be working together and that my oldest and her youngest were the same age. Needless to say, we clicked pretty quickly and discovered that we had a lot in common, from coffee and gin drinking to singing and running – to say I'd met my soul sister was an understatement. Vicki is my rock and I honestly don't know what I would do without her. I feel like I've known her all my life and I'm proud of everything that she does.

Not only is Vicki a military wife and mother, she's also a military daughter, has been posted all over the world ever since she was a baby and has only just recently settled in a civilian house. Her dad was a major in the SASC (Small Arms School Corps), and one of the first postings she remembers properly was when they lived in Hong Kong. Vicki was five and her brother Joe was three. Her mum Debs had help in the form of a lovely local lady called Margaret, and every Saturday Margaret would make lunch for Debs and the kids which was a simple fried rice dish with vegetables and an omelette. This simple dish became a firm family favourite which Debs would make often wherever they were posted as it was quick to prepare, she knew the kids would eat it and it was a reminder of their time in Hong Kong and of the love that was was shown to the family by Margaret.

Ham, chicken or prawns can of course be added as well as any vegetables that you may have to hand. Debs was surprised to find out that there was no garlic in the dish. I like to make fried rice on Monday night if there's any meat left over in the fridge from Sunday's roast. Chicken, ham, beef, pork all work beautifully as well as prawns and tuna. I like to add some spring onions or crispy salad onions for flavour and texture, and some chilli for a bit of a kick.

Margaret, Joe and Vicki in Hong Kong

SERVES 4

4 eggs

2 tbsp oil

salt and pepper

300g cooked rice, chilled

1 onion, roughly chopped

250g mixed vegetables – peas, carrots, sweetcorn

3 tbsp soy sauce

prep: 15 minutes, cook: 15 minutes)

Place a large frying pan over a medium heat. Beat the eggs with a pinch of salt and pepper. Add ½ tablespoon of oil to the pan then add the eggs. Cook until just set, like a plain omelette. Transfer onto a chopping board, roll it up and chop into small pieces.

Heat the rest of the oil in the pan and cook the onions until slightly golden and soft. Add the vegetables and rice, mix well to combine and cook until hot. Add the chopped up omelette and soy sauce, stir and serve.

GAME DAY LAYERED DIP

This is another recipe for a dip that never fails to impress a crowd and was suggested to me as the possible officers' wives' dip recipe when I started researching. I also wanted to include this recipe in the book as it's a great dip to take over to someone's house for a social gathering or to enjoy while watching rugby or any sporting event on television. You can leave out the bacon if you want to make it vegetarian and I've also had a similar layered dip with a layer of beef chilli added … which, I have to say, tasted out of this world.

SERVES 4-6

1 tbsp oil

1 small onion, finely chopped

½ green pepper, finely chopped

1 garlic clove, finely chopped or crushed

6 rashers of smoky streaky bacon, roughly chopped

1-2 tbsp pickled jalapeño pepper slices, roughly chopped

1 tsp smoked paprika

200g cream cheese

3 tbsp mayonnaise

2 tbsp sour cream

1 tsp garlic granules

salt and pepper to season

75g Red Leicester cheese, grated

1 big bag of tortilla chips to serve

prep: 15 minutes, cook: 20 minutes

Place a small frying pan over a medium heat, add the oil and sauté the onion and green pepper for about 5 minutes until they start to soften. Add the chopped/crushed garlic and chopped bacon and continue to sauté until the bacon starts to crisp, then remove from the heat to cool.

In a small bowl, mix together the cream cheese, mayonnaise, sour cream, smoked paprika and garlic granules. Stir in the jalapeño peppers and taste to check the seasoning, adding salt and pepper if required. Scrape the cream cheese mixture into an oven proof dish, measuring roughly 20cm square, and smooth it out to a nice level layer in the bottom of the dish. Top the cream cheese with the vegetable and bacon mixture and spread it out evenly. Finish by scattering the grated cheese on top to cover the bottom two layers.

Bake the dip in a preheated oven set to 160°C fan/180°C/gas mark 4 for 15-20 minutes. Leave to cool for 5 minutes before serving with tortilla chips and call a couple of friends to help you enjoy it.

LAMB & VEGETABLE SUET PUDDINGS

My uncle Robin served in tanks with the Army in the 1970s and 1980s, and one of his postings took him, Aunty Heulwen and my cousins Tina and Ann to Germany for a couple of years. It's great hearing their experiences as a military family and I know that they love the fact that I am now following in their footsteps by being part of the military community too.

Aunty Heulwen is one heck of a cook and used to own and run a very popular café in Swansea which I loved to visit and help out as much as possible when I was a little girl. I know that when they lived in Germany, they embraced their surroundings and culture and would eat whatever was available for them to buy from the local shops, with Heulwen cooking meals from home as well as trying out new German dishes when she could.

Although Heulwen is fluent in both Welsh and English, she hadn't quite got to grips with speaking German and would mainly point at different things she wanted to buy and say 'danke' when she was happy with her purchases. On one of Heulwen's first visits to the local butcher's shop she pointed at some meat that she thought was beef and bought it. She went home happy with her purchase, cooked it for the family and they all devoured it.

A trip to purchase the same meat would occur weekly, until one day she noticed another nice bit of meat on display in the cabinet and asked the butcher what it was. 'Beef,' he replied in his best English. 'Oh,' Heulwen was confused. She pointed at the meat she'd been feeding to her family for the last few weeks and asked, 'So what's that then …?'

'Horse,' came the reply.

Adapting to new surroundings, making sure that the family settle in and that the new house quickly becomes a home is something that is part and parcel of being married to someone in the forces. You take everything in your stride and try and enjoy every moment before you have to pack up and move on to the next adventure. It's not an easy thing to do, time and time again, but it's something that you'll happily do for your partner because you love them, and you want to support them.

This recipe is something that my cousin Ann remembers Aunty Heulwen cooking for them when they lived in Germany and it's not what I was expecting her to say, but I can understand why it stood out for her as a recipe and a memory of their time in Germany, because it was comfort food that reminded them of home.

Suet puddings aren't as popular now as they once were, but they're so tasty and not at all difficult to make. You don't have to use 'proper' suet if you don't fancy it, there's great vegetarian suet available from the shops that tastes just as good. Please don't be put off by the long list of ingredients, because it's worth the effort.

SERVES 6

320g self-raising flour

160g suet

1 x tsp salt

ground black pepper to taste

1 x tsp finely chopped fresh
rosemary

cold water

FILLING

400g lamb neck fillet, cut into
small chunks

1 x small leek

1 x carrot

¼ medium swede

1 x medium potato

salt and pepper

oil for browning

GRAVY

water from the vegetables

lamb bones

2 onions

2 carrots

2 celery sticks

salt and pepper to taste

2 tbsp oil

1 couple sprigs of rosemary

a bulb of garlic

a glug of red wine

2 tsp redcurrant jelly

1-2 tbsps plain flour or corn
flour

gravy browning (optional)

prep: 40 minutes, cook: 1 hour

Prepare the filling for the pudding by chopping up the leek, carrot, swede and potato to roughly 1½ cm cubes, and par-boil in salted water. Retain the vegetable water for the gravy. Cut the meat into 2cm pieces, season and brown in a frying pan before setting to one side to cool. Don't overcook – brown the meat in a hot pan so that it's coloured slightly but still raw on the inside as they will continue to cook in the pudding. Keep the pan with the meat juices for the gravy.

Grease a pudding basin and place a small disc of greaseproof paper on the bottom and set to one side. While the vegetables and meat are cooling, make the pastry by sifting the flour into a large bowl then add the salt, pepper and rosemary and mix. Add the suet and distribute evenly throughout the flour then gradually add water until the dough forms a ball and comes away from the side of the bowl. Tip the dough onto a lightly floured surface and knead until smooth. Cut ⅓ off the dough and put it to one side for the lid. Roll out the remaining dough into a circle large enough to fill the pudding basin. Carefully lift the pastry and line the basin making sure that it fits into the corners and overlaps the top slightly.

Mix the vegetables and meat together in a bowl and season slightly before filling the pastry-lined basin. Roll out the remaining piece of pastry to fit the top of the pudding; wet the edges and stick the lid on top trimming away any excess pastry. Place a disc of greased silicone paper on top and then 2 sheets of foil, overlapping in the middle so that the pastry can expand during cooking. Tie the foil in place around the rim of the basin with string and create a little handle so that you can easily lift the pudding in and out of the saucepan. Place a small saucer into a large saucepan and fill halfway up with boiling water over a medium heat. Place the pudding into the saucepan and cover with the lid and steam for 1½-1¾ hours, topping up the water throughout the cooking time if it evaporates too quickly.

While the pudding is steaming, make the gravy by cutting the onions, carrots and celery into large pieces and place along with the lamb bones, rosemary and garlic into a baking tray. Season, drizzle with oil and roast for 45-60 minutes. After this time, scrape the juices, bones and vegetables into the frying pan with the browned meat juices and deglaze with some red wine. Add the vegetable water and reduce until the liquid starts to thicken, adding cornflour or plain flour to thicken and gravy browning to add colour if needed. Strain the liquid away from the bones and vegetables into another saucepan and continue to thicken. Check the seasoning at this point and adjust if necessary as well as adding a teaspoon of redcurrant jelly. Keep warm until the pudding is ready.

Once the pudding has steamed carefully remove from the saucepan, remove the string, foil and greaseproof paper and turn out onto a plate. Serve with the gravy and some roast rosemary potatoes and green peas.

MAM'S FISH CHOWDER

Of all the countries my husband has visited during his career, from Bosnia, Iraq and Afghanistan to Cyprus, Canada and Germany, it's Norway's majestic landscape, people and food that has left the biggest impression.

It was around 2001, quite early on in his military career, when Matt was sent to Norway with the Grenadier Guards as part of a three-week summer exercise. I think, at the time, he didn't realise how much of an impact the country would have on him, especially as on his return he went straight into training to be deployed to Northern Ireland which was the first of a long line of tours for him. He just keeps saying how stunning the Norwegian mountains were – beautiful, endless peaks with clear, cool, refreshing water drunk straight from the streams.

I think youth and innocence were on his side when he was in Norway. He hadn't yet experienced all that war would throw at him. His young wide-eyed wonderment has held that pure, innocent memory of Norway so clear in his mind, which I think is wonderful, especially knowing what he went through afterwards.

SERVES 4-6

1 tbsp butter

1 tbsp oil

2 large carrots, peeled and cut into small 1cm pieces

3 celery sticks, finely chopped

1 leek, cleaned and finely chopped

½ celeriac, cut into small 1cm cubes

300g waxy potatoes, peeled and cut into 1cm cubes

small bunch of parsley stalks

2 tbsp plain flour

1 tsp curry powder

1½ litres stock, either fish, chicken or vegetable

400g white fish like haddock, cod, pollock or smoked haddock

½ lemon

300ml double cream

salt and white pepper to taste

cayenne pepper to serve

small bunch of fresh chives to serve

prep: 20 minutes, cook: 30 minutes

Heat the butter and oil in a large pan over a medium heat and add the chopped carrots, leek, celeriac, potatoes and parsley stalks. Cover so that the vegetables can sweat. Cook for 10 minutes, stirring occasionally until the vegetables are soft.

Add the curry powder and flour and stir before adding the stock and stirring again. Leave the mixture to simmer and thicken for another 10 minutes. Taste before seasoning with salt and pepper. Cut the fish into 2cm pieces and add to the pan along with the lemon. After 3-4 minutes, add the cream and cayenne pepper, stir, taste and serve with some snipped chives on top.

BOSNIAN BUREK

I love listening to Matt's stories of the places he's visited; what he did, what the weather was like and what food he ate. We met in 2007, a month after he was medevacked out of Afghanistan. That tour was going to be his last in a long line of tours with the Grenadier Guards.

A few years before Afghanistan he was in Bosnia for a six-month tour during winter. Now my husband doesn't get cold – that's my job – but he still says to this day that he has never been as cold as he was in Bosnia. The weather made this tour even more difficult and felt longer than it was, especially when they were in the mountains in deep snow up over their knees.

He loves to reminisce about when they were in Sarajevo and would go and treat themselves to some street food at the end of duties, with the Bosnian burek being a favourite choice of snack. This is a local equivalent of a Cornish pasty – a deliciously flaky filo pastry spiral filled with spiced minced meat and served hot.

Its simplicity is beautiful, especially by using shop-bought filo pastry and served with some good quality yoghurt. You could easily use minced lamb or chicken and add other spices like ground cumin, coriander and chilli. Before experimenting though, follow the recipe below for the authentic taste of Sarajevo on a cold winter's night.

MAKES 6-8

500g good quality minced beef

2 large onions, finely chopped

2 eggs

2 tablespoons paprika

salt and pepper

150g melted unsalted butter

6 sheets filo pastry

prep: 30 minutes, cook: 45 minutes

Preheat the oven to 160°C fan/180°C/gas mark 4.

In a large bowl, mix together the minced beef, finely chopped onions, eggs, paprika, salt and pepper.

To assemble the burek, brush one sheet of filo with melted butter all over and place a line of the mince mixture along the long edge of the pastry, leaving a 3cm gap from the edge. Fold this edge over the meat and continue to roll the pastry up to form a long sausage. Starting from one end, roll the pastry into a pinwheel or a snail shell and place onto a baking tray lined with greaseproof paper. Repeat with the remaining filo pastry sheets and meat.

You can either make individual bureks, or make one large wheel by adding the next filo pastry sausage to the first and continuing the spiral. Once all the meat has been used up, brush the top of the burek with more melted butter and bake in the oven for about 40-45 minutes, or until golden brown.

Serve the individual bureks or cut wedges of the larger burek along with some yoghurt.

DRESSED POTATO SALAD

This is a staple recipe when it comes to barbecues in our family. My great aunt Irene would make the best potato salad which was similar to this, but didn't include the mustard, bratwurst or red pepper. It always goes down well with guests and is something that can be made ahead and kept covered in the fridge until needed. The addition of the brats and pepper is in order to bulk out the dish and make use of some leftover ingredients that you may have.

This is another adaptable recipe to suit your fridge contents, and something that works well if you need to eat things up before being posted, but it's also a great recipe to have in your armoury for summer entertaining or if you're asked to bring a dish to a party or a social gathering on the patch.

SERVES 6

500g new potatoes, cleaned
    and cut in half

2 large eggs

1 tsp vinegar

½ tbsp Dijon mustard

1 tbsp mayonnaise

cold, cooked bratwursts or
    sausages

4 spring onions

50g pickled gherkins, plus
    some of the pickling liquid

½ red pepper

salt and pepper to taste

a small bunch of chives

prep: 20 minutes, cook: 15 minutes

Boil the new potatoes in salted water for about 15 minutes until cooked and tender. Drain, and return the potatoes to the pan.

While the potatoes are cooking, boil the eggs with the vinegar until hard boiled – about 10 minutes. Drain and submerge the eggs in cold water to cool.

Cut the cold brats or sausages lengthways then diagonally into pieces about 2cm long. Top and tail the spring onions and cut diagonally, about 1cm long. Chop the gherkins into 1cm cubes along with the red pepper. Place all the ingredients, including the mustard and mayonnaise into the pan with the warm potatoes.

Peel and roughly chop the egg into 2cm pieces and add to the pan, giving everything a gentle stir to combine. Taste to check the seasoning, adding a little salt and pepper if required. Add a little pickle liquid to help coat the potatoes with the dressing.

Snip the chives on top and serve. It's great for a picnic or as a side dish for a barbecue.

FRIDGE RAID TRAY BAKE

This recipe makes a weekly appearance in our house. It's easy and tasty and you can use whatever vegetables, meat, pulses and even cheese that you have to hand – and for extra flavour, you can travel the world with this one-tray wonder, depending what spices you add.

This recipe comes into its own when you're posted away and waiting for your stuff to arrive at the house, or when your stuff has been shipped onwards ahead of the move, and all you have is some basic kit to use. All this recipe requires is a knife, a chopping board – although a plate will do – and a baking tray or oven dish. And that's it.

It's such a versatile dish that pretty much anything goes – it's just as easy to make a version with meat as it is to go completely vegan or vegetarian. This is also a relatively quick meal to throw together, and while it's in the oven you can do other things like the washing or have a sit down and a glass of gin!

SERVES 4

1 sweet potato

2 old potatoes, Maris Piper or similar

2 onions

1 courgette

4 large tomatoes

1 yellow pepper

5 garlic cloves

olive oil

salt and pepper

smoked paprika

ground cumin

1 tin chickpeas or 8 sausages

150g feta cheese

prep: 15 minutes, cook: 40 minutes

Preheat the oven to 190°C fan/210°C/gas mark 6-7.

Wash and roughly chop the potatoes into 2-3cm/1-inch chunks and place into a baking tray or large oven dish. Peel and cut the onions into 8ths and add to the tray. Chop the peppers into similar sized pieces to the potatoes and cut the tomatoes into quarters.

Cut the courgette lengthways in half and then into chunky semi-circles, about 2cm thick and peel the garlic cloves and leave whole.

Add everything to the baking tray and drizzle over a little oil, season with salt and pepper and sprinkle over about 2 teaspoons each of the smoked paprika and ground cumin. Give everything a good mix with your hand and then pop the tray into the oven for 20 minutes.

After this time, give the vegetables a quick stir and if using sausages, add them now before popping the tray back into the oven for a further 20 minutes. Then stir the vegetables again and, if using chickpeas instead of sausages, add them now or turn the sausages and pop back into the oven for 15 minutes.

Crumble in the feta cheese and bake for a further 5 minutes before serving.

TIPS:

If you don't have any spices apart from salt and oil, then that's fine – the vegetables will taste delicious regardless. Other spices you can use are fajitas spice mix, curry powder, Cajun, ras el hanout, mixed herbs … anything you fancy. Other vegetables you can add are cauliflower, broccoli, aubergine, squash, pumpkin, mushrooms, red onions, any coloured pepper, carrots, swede, parsnips … you get the idea. Meat-wise, sausages are a favourite and you can easily use veggie sausages if you prefer. How about chicken breasts or thighs, pork chops, any white fish or salmon? Just adjust the cooking times as these will take less time to cook, especially the fish. Make the tray bake something you and your family will enjoy eating and I guarantee that it will be used time and time again.

HASH

This recipe is one of those that works for breakfast, lunch or supper and is a great way of using up leftovers as well as keeping the dishwashing to a minimum. Corned beef hash is a forces' classic that's on the menu in many cookhouses. It needs minimal ingredients but is a tasty and filling meal to serve to the troops.

I'm a fan of hash as you only need one pan and it's quick to make. It's another great recipe to have in your armoury if you're waiting to be posted and have little kitchen kit to use.

Hash, in my eyes, needs to have potatoes and onions in there to be called hash – and yes there's a similarity to bubble and squeak, although that's refried vegetables left over from a Sunday roast, whereas hash is more of a brunch dish that includes meat and potentially a crispy fried egg. Much like my fridge raid tray bake recipe, you can use up whatever you have in the fridge to make this dish, however, below I've written the recipe as if I'd bought all the ingredients to make it to my ideal specifications.

SERVES 4

2½ tbsp olive oil

3-4 old potatoes, peeled and diced into 2cm cubes

1 large or 2 small onions

1 green pepper

8-10 smoky bacon rashers or leftover roast beef, chopped into 2cm cubes

2-3 garlic cloves, crushed

salt and pepper

4 eggs

prep: 15 minutes, cook: 20 minutes

Parboil the potatoes in boiling salted water for 5 minutes then drain and keep them to one side. Roughly chop the onions and peppers into 2 cm pieces and cut the bacon to roughly the same size.

Heat 1½ tablespoons of oil in a large frying pan, add the onions and peppers and sauté for a couple of minutes over a medium heat until they start to soften. Add the parboiled potatoes and continue to sauté until the potatoes and vegetables start to catch some colour and crisp up. Add the bacon and crushed garlic and cook until the bacon is crispy. Season with the salt and pepper and keep warm while frying the eggs.

Heat the remaining oil in a small frying pan and fry the eggs until crispy underneath and with a runny yolk. Divide the hash between 4 plates and add an egg on top, with plenty of tomato ketchup on the side.

CHAPTER 7

HOMECOMING

The day that they actually come home sends you into a complete spin. Your emotions are all over the place, going from giddy excitement to sheer panic so much so, that you don't remember what they look like. You're also having to manage two children who are very excited and ask you every five minutes 'When is Daddy coming home?'. I always say to my husband that I won't believe he's actually home until he's landed in this country somewhere and is en route back to camp, and even then I don't really believe it until I see him and I get completely squashed in one of his massive bear hugs.

While they're away you almost bottle up your emotions and keep yourself extra busy doing everything and anything possible to occupy yourself and the children. And then when you do see them, you're sort of numb and unsure of how to react. It takes me a good few weeks to adjust to having him home, disrupting the good routine the girls are so used to, whipping them up into a frenzy of silliness at every opportunity and just generally getting in the way.

One of my coping mechanisms is cooking. It calms my thoughts and centres my emotions. It has an ability to focus my busy brain and channel any worries into what I'm cooking. It's also one way that I can show my husband how much I love him and how much I've missed him, and even if my head hasn't quite figured out that he's now home, my cooking and the sentiment behind cooking him his favourite meal shows him exactly how I'm feeling.

Having him home is a celebration and usually involves a big social gathering with the family, so this chapter is full of dishes to enjoy around the table as a family again, sharing stories, laughing and getting to know each other after months apart, longing for his safe return.

ROAST CHICKEN WITH CORN & HASSELBACK POTATOES

Roast dinner is one of those things that evokes thoughts of home and comfort. It's the meal that I always look forward to eating if I've been away working, and no one makes it better than my mother. My husband even prefers my mother's roast chicken dinner to mine. This is a relatively simple dish to make as I'm not making gravy and all the trimmings, but rather, serving up some crunchy Hasselback potatoes, stir-fried kale and charred corn on the cob.

Nan once told me a wonderful story about when she got some corn on the cob during rationing …

Nan and her sister Vera often joined queues for rations even if they didn't need anything, it's just what everyone did. Word spread quickly whenever the local shop got something in and before you knew it, there was a queue of people waiting to buy whatever was in stock using some of their precious ration coupons.

One day, Nan and Vera followed the crowd and queued to get whatever was on offer, which proved to be corn on the cob – something neither of them had cooked or eaten before. The sisters asked for advice from others in the queue as to what to do with the vegetable, but it seemed that many others were in the same boat and didn't have a clue how to cook or eat it. On the way home, Nan and Vera got a tram and the very friendly driver told them to boil the corn. Well, they hadn't thought to ask for how long they would need to cook it, so they boiled it for a couple of hours …

Needless to say, neither of them enjoyed their first taste of corn on the cob.

SERVES 4

1 large whole chicken

2 tbsp olive oil

salt and pepper

1 bulb of garlic, cut in half

1 lemon, cut in half

bunch of fresh herbs: thyme, rosemary, bay, parsley …

4 cobs of corn

60g butter

prep: 30 minutes, cook: 2 hours

Preheat the oven to 170°C fan/190°C/gas mark 5. Place the chicken into a large roasting tin, drizzle over the oil and season with plenty of salt and pepper. Place one half of the lemon and one half of the garlic along with half of the herbs inside the chicken's cavity. Tuck the other halves around the chicken and drizzle with a little oil and a sprinkle of salt.

Roast for about 1¾ hours, but double-check the cooking instructions on the pack as this will vary depending on the size of the chicken.

Wash and dry the potatoes, then place them one at a time onto a wooden soon, this will help you slice through them with a sharp knife. Cut the potatoes lengthways into 3mm slices.

In a large saucepan over a medium heat, melt the butter and oil and place the prepared potatoes into the pan, spooning over the frothing butter and oil, coating each of them in turn. Turn them over so that they get a good covering and start to warm through. Move the potatoes from the pan to a baking tray along with the butter and bake in the oven for the last 30 minutes of the chicken cooking time. Once the chicken is ready and out of the oven, increase the heat to

HASSELBACK POTATOES & KALE

6 medium potatoes

a good knob of butter

2 tbsp oil

salt and pepper

bag of kale or spring greens

2-3 garlic cloves

½-1 red chilli

juice and zest of ½ orange

200°C fan/220°C/gas mark 7 and continue to cook the potatoes for a further 20 minutes, or until cooked in the middle and crispy on the outside.

While the chicken and potatoes are busy cooking, parboil the corn in some salted water for no more than 5 minutes (unlike my nan). After this time, drain the water and colour the corn on a griddle pan or in a frying pan – or better still, on a barbecue with a little butter and some salt. When it's nicely coloured all over, it's ready.

If you fancy something green to serve with the dish, just sauté some spring greens or kale in some olive oil with fresh chilli and garlic and finish them with some sea salt and some toasted almonds or hazelnuts. A grating of orange zest and a squeeze of the juice will bring the whole thing to life.

Slice the breast meat and spoon over some of the cooking juices from the roasting tin. Serve with the charred corn, crunchy Hasselbacks and vibrant greens.

Don't be tempted to eat the leg, thigh or wing meat – save this and make my buffalo chicken dip on page 176 or the chicken pie on page 170.

HONEY ROAST HAM & PARSLEY SAUCE

You know when you're away from home and you dream of a good home-cooked meal made lovingly for you by your mam or loved one? Well this is mine and the one I got most excited about whenever I went home to visit my parents when we lived in London. It's not fancy, and quite traditional, but what makes it that special 'welcome-home' meal, is the parsley sauce. It's so comforting, slightly sweet and balances the meat beautifully – plus Mam always made it with love, and you can't get any better than that can you?

The sauce should just be spooned sparingly over the meat, but in our family we drown our plate with the parsley goodness like gravy on a Sunday roast and Dad is the worst at doing this. He usually loses the ham under all the sauce and because there's so much left over after he's eaten everything, he 'has' to mop it up with some bread otherwise it would be a waste wouldn't it?

We introduced Matt to this meal, probably early on in our relationship when I brought him home every so often. He loves it so much that when he comes home after weeks or months away with work, this is his first meal request. He says that he prefers mine to my mam's, of course, but I know he's lying because Mam's is the best.

SERVES 6-8

2kg ham

1 leek, cleaned and trimmed

2 carrots

2 celery sticks

2 bay leaves

2 sprigs of rosemary

1 tbsp peppercorns

GLAZE

85g honey

2 tbsp dark-brown sugar

1 tsp mustard powder

½ tsp ground cloves

1 sprig of rosemary, finely chopped

prep: 40 minutes, cook: 2 hours

Roughly chop the leek, carrots and celery sticks. Place the ham into a large saucepan along with the chopped vegetables, bay leaves, rosemary and peppercorns and cover with cold water. Bring to the boil then reduce to a simmer, cover and leave to bubble for about 1 hour 20 minutes.

After this time, remove the ham from the pan and place into a foil-lined baking tray. In a small bowl, mix together all the glaze ingredients, remove the skin from the ham and score the fat down to the meat with a sharp knife – you can just do diagonal stripes or diamonds, it's up to you. Brush or pour the glaze onto the ham, making sure that the fat is covered with the honey mixture. Bake in a preheated oven set to 180°C fan/200°C/gas mark 6 for 20 minutes, then spoon the glaze and juices over the meat and return to the oven for a further 15 minutes. Baste with the juices once more before roasting for a final 10 minutes. Remove from the oven and rest for 20 minutes before slicing.

Make the parsley sauce by melting the butter in a medium pan and add the flour. Stir to create a paste and gradually add the milk, stirring continuously until all the milk has been added and you have a thick white sauce. Reduce the heat to low, roughly chop the parsley and add to the sauce along with a couple of tablespoons of the sweet roasting juice from the ham. You can add more of this wonderful cooking liquid to make a thinner sauce and to add extra flavour. Taste to check seasoning adding salt and some black pepper if needed.

PARSLEY SAUCE

30g butter

30g plain flour

350ml milk

small bunch fresh parsley, roughly chopped

2-3 tbsp of the meat juice after roasting

salt and pepper to taste

Serve the roast ham with some buttery mash, green beans and any other vegetables you fancy with a good spoonful or 5 of the parsley sauce.

Tip: Please don't go throwing that delicious cooking liquid down the drain because that is effectively the tastiest stock ever and will make the most amazing vegetable soup. Just add whatever vegetables you have and cook until soft, then blitz until smooth. The easiest soup would be a bag of frozen peas added, blitzed and finished with a little cream. Delicious.

What can you do with any leftover ham? Well, it will make the most delicious ham sandwiches, or ham fried rice but in our family, we eat it cold with some boiled and buttered potatoes and pickled beetroot.

CHOCOLATE ORANGE DOUBLE DRIZZLE CAKE

It's difficult to describe the emotions that you feel when your loved one is due back home. It's a mixture of emotions: joy, certainly, but also a strong anxiety. Time stands still on the actual day, not helped with the timings never quite working out as promised, with delays happening on a regular basis. You have to manage your own expectations as well as any little troopers that might be counting down the sleeps until Daddy or Mummy gets home. I've learnt that it's best to be vague and to never give an exact day or time.

Distraction techniques go into overdrive for the whole duration they're away of course, but even more so on the day they arrive back and, true to form, you'll find me in the kitchen cooking or baking to keep busy, but also to make sure there's something homemade and delicious ready and waiting. My husband is a fan of chocolate orange and so, this double drizzle cake never disappoints. The double drizzle come from the orange syrup drizzle as well as a chocolate ganache drizzle … any excuse for a bit of ganache, if I'm honest.

It's a relatively simple cake to make, but there are a couple of elements to work through – I find this helps pass the time while the clock ticks slowly on the wall.

SERVES 8-10

225g butter

225g caster sugar

225g self-raising flour

4 eggs

50g ground almonds

zest of 1 orange

juice of ½ orange

ORANGE DRIZZLE & CANDIED PEEL

75ml orange juice (juice of ½-1 orange)

75g caster sugar, plus additional for dusting the candied peel

peel of ½ orange

prep: 25 minutes, cook: 1 hour

Grease and line an 20cm/8-inch square, loose bottomed tin. Preheat the oven to 160°C fan/180°C /gas mark 4.

Cream the butter and sugar until light and fluffy. Beat the eggs in, one at a time, adding some flour towards the end to help stop the mixture curdling. Add the ground almonds and then the remaining flour. Stir in the orange zest and juice, making sure that the mixture is evenly combined before pouring into the prepared tin. Smooth the top of the mixture, then bake in the oven for about 45-55 minutes. The cake is ready when an inserted skewer comes out clean.

While the cake is baking, make the candied peel and orange drizzle so that you can use it as soon as the cake is out of the oven. To make the candied peel, remove the peel from the orange and cut it into strips measuring 0.5cm by 4cm, then place in a small saucepan and cover with water. Bring to the boil and let it bubble for 10-15 seconds before removing it from the heat. Drain, saving the peel in a sieve, then return it to the saucepan and add 75g of caster sugar with 75ml of orange juice. Bring to the boil for 3-5 minutes until the liquid is syrupy. Remove the peel, but save the syrup to drizzle over the cake. Dust the peel in some caster sugar before leaving to cool and dry on a wire rack.

CHOCOLATE GANACHE DRIZZLE

100g dark chocolate

80ml double cream

When the cake has baked, remove from the oven and while it's still in its tin, poke a couple of holes into it using a skewer or cocktail stick, then drizzle or spoon the orange syrup all over the surface, letting it absorb into the cake. Leave the cake to cool completely before removing from the tin, then pop it on a plate, ready to be decorated.

To make the ganache, break the chocolate into chunks and place them in a bowl over a saucepan of simmering water. Let the chocolate start to melt before adding the cream and stirring until you have a smooth glossy ganache. Remove the bowl from the saucepan and leave to cool slightly before drizzling the ganache over the cake. I find this easier when the ganache is in a piping bag, but you can pour it straight from the bowl or use a spoon if you prefer. To finish, decorate with the candied orange peel.

ROAST TOMATO SOUP & CHEESY CHOUX PUFFS

Tomato soup is a mess function staple that would make an appearance as a starter at many dinners for all ranks of the armed forces. It's a soup that has humble beginnings but is full flavoured and comforting. The American tradition of having a bowl of tomato soup with a grilled cheese sandwich screams home comfort to me. Serving the same flavour, but in a different way, instantly elevates it to be grand enough for an officers' dinner or even for a prime minister.

Reading through some of the dishes that Winston Churchill ate during his time at Number 10, I came across countless soups, many of which were made using simple ingredients. I then came across a recipe for beignets with cheese, made by deep frying choux pastry with cheese - absolutely divine. This inspired me to replace the American grilled cheese sandwich with a batch of cheesy choux puffs, which are essentially the same as Churchill's beignets, but baked rather than fried.

SERVES 4

2 red onions

3 large garlic cloves

2 large carrots

800g tomatoes – a mixture of cherry and plum.

salt and sugar to taste

2 tbsp olive oil

CHEESY CHOUX PUFFS

75g plain flour

½ tsp salt

½ tsp cayenne pepper

¾ tsp mustard powder

60g butter

150ml water

2 medium eggs

100g Gruyère cheese, grated

50g Parmesan cheese, grated

prep: 30 minutes, cook: 40 minutes

Preheat the oven to 160°C fan/180°C/gas mark 4, roughly chop the onion and carrot and place them in a roasting tray with a pinch of salt and a drizzle of oil, then roast in the oven for 20 minutes. Roughly chop the tomatoes and add them, along with the peeled garlic cloves, to the tray in the oven after the 20 minutes. Add another pinch of salt and a good pinch of sugar, give everything a good stir and pop back into the oven for another 20 minutes.

By now, the vegetables should be soft and sweet. Scrape everything into a food processor. Use some boiling water to persuade all the sticky bits of flavour out of the roasting tin and into the processor.

Add more water to the vegetables and blitz until smooth. Add enough water to slacken the mixture and taste to check the seasoning. For a really smooth consistency you can also pass the soup through a sieve.

To make the cheesy choux puffs, preheat the oven to 200°C fan/220°C/gas mark 7 and line two baking sheets with greaseproof paper. Turn the paper upside down and mark out circles using a pencil and a 4cm round cutter. Fill the two sheets with circles but leave a gap between each one.

Sieve the flour, salt, cayenne pepper and mustard powder onto a large sheet of greaseproof paper; this will make it easier to add it to the hot liquid once the butter has melted. Heat the water and butter in a saucepan until the butter has melted and the water starts to bubble; do not let the liquid boil as it will evaporate. Take the saucepan off the heat and add the flour mixture straight away, beating together until a thick dough or paste forms. Put the saucepan back to the heat for a minute to cook out the flour, then scrape the mixture into a bowl and leave to cool slightly.

The soup shouldn't be too thick or too thin – it should coat the back of a spoon easily.

While the dough is cooling, beat the eggs and prepare a piping bag with a 1cm nozzle; if you don't have a nozzle you can just snip a 1cm hole in the bag. I use a pint glass or a jug to stand my piping bags in as I usually bake on my own with no one to hold the bag for me.

After about 5 minutes, gradually add a little of the egg to the dough and beat well with a wooden spoon. The mixture always looks like it doesn't want to combine; but persevere as it will eventually come together. Continue to beat until all the egg has been added. Mix the grated cheeses and add most of it to the mixture, reserving 25g to sprinkle on top of the choux puffs before they're baked.

Fill the piping bag with the warm dough and pipe rounds of it onto the already prepared baking sheets. Get a little cup of water, wet a finger and dab the tops of the dough mounds if they've peaked where you've piped them. Sprinkle a little extra cheese on top of each mound and a little water around them. This will create steam while they bake and give you crispy choux puffs.

Bake for 15 minutes then, without opening the oven door, reduce the temperature to 170°C fan/190°C/gas mark 5 and bake for a further 15 minutes until golden brown. Remove from the oven and serve warm with the roast tomato soup.

LEFTOVER CHICKEN PIE

When Matt and I started dating, chicken pie was a regular weekly meal that I happily made for us to enjoy, usually on a Monday or a Tuesday night as a way of using chicken left over from Sunday's roast. We always had it with mash and peas and it never failed to satisfy and comfort us after a long day at work. I've never written the recipe down as I just made the pastry and used whatever vegetables we had along with either leftover roast chicken or baked ham – or both.

I always tend to have onions, carrots and celery in the fridge and often have mushrooms too. Add to these, some herbs, a glug of white wine, some chicken stock, with a little plain flour to thicken and that is the basis of my pie filling. I almost always make too much filling when I make the pie, so I keep the rest and eat it with rice as another evening meal. The pastry is a straightforward shortcrust that can be used for savoury or sweet pies, so freeze any offcuts or make some jam tarts just like my nan would do. I don't make this pie as often as I used to, but that makes it even more special and a treat when I do.

SERVES 6

250g plain flour

150g fat – either 75g each of
    lard and butter or all butter

1 egg

a good pinch of salt

enough cold water to bind

PIE FILLING

1 tbsp oil

leftover chicken or baked ham,
    roughly chopped

4 rashers of smoked bacon

1 onion

1 carrot

2 celery sticks

150g mushrooms, roughly
    chopped

2 garlic cloves

a good glug of white wine

1 tsp dried thyme

1 tbsp plain flour

500ml chicken stock

salt and pepper to season

a little cream to add richness
    (optional)

prep: 30 minutes, cook: 1 hour

The pastry can be made beforehand. Use any spare 5 minutes to make it, then wrap in cling film and place in the fridge until needed. You can make the pastry by hand by rubbing the fats into the flour and salt until it resembles breadcrumbs. Add the egg and mix with a knife and gradually add the water a little at a time until the dough comes together. Shape into a ball, wrap and store in the fridge.

To make the pastry in a food processor, pulse the flour and fats until they look like breadcrumbs. Add the egg and the water a little at a time while pulsing the processor, stopping as soon as the dough forms a ball. Wrap in clingfilm and keep in the fridge until needed.

Prepare the filling by sweating the onions, carrots and celery together in a little oil until soft. Add the meat and cook for 2 minutes. Add the garlic, mushrooms and thyme, then the wine and cook for a couple of minutes. Add a tablespoon of flour and then gradually add some stock until the liquid is thick but not too thick. Any excess liquid can be used as additional sauce for the pie when serving it. Cook the mixture for a few more minutes, taste to check the seasoning and adjust as necessary. Add the cream right at the end, stir and then leave to one side away from the heat while you preheat the oven to 180°C fan/200°C/gas mark 6 and prepare the pastry.

I use a 7-inch loose-bottom cake tin to make my pie as it's the perfect size for at least two suppers for both of us, and having a loose bottom means that the pie will come out of the tin easily. Grease the tin with a little butter before rolling out the pastry to the thickness of a pound coin. Lift the pastry carefully using the rolling pin and fit it snugly to the tin. Trim the edges using a knife and roll out another round of pastry for the lid.

Serve with buttery mash and peas

To fill the pie, use a slotted spoon to lift out the meat and vegetables into the pastry, then add a little liquid at the end – you don't want the pie to be too wet. Any liquid left over can be poured as a sauce after serving.

Brush the edge of the pastry with beaten egg before placing the lid on top. Seal the edges by gently, but firmly pressing them together then trim off any excess. Crimp the edges using your fingers then cut at least one hole in the middle of the pie to let out any steam. Glaze the pie with yet more beaten egg then bake in the oven for 35-40 minutes until golden brown. Leave to rest for at least 15 minutes before cutting it. This will give you extra time to sort out the vegetables, mash the potatoes and heat up any left-over juices that didn't make it into the pie.

RASPBERRY, ROSE & PISTACHIO VICTORIA SPONGE

Cakes were a rare treat during rationing as eggs were scarce and the butter allowance was small. Exceptions were always made for wedding and birthday cakes when ingredients were saved, begged or borrowed, but even then, the flavours and decorations weren't anything extravagant.

In order to conserve fuel, the Ministry of Food encouraged that baked goods should be cooked at the same time as a roast meat or a pie. Neighbours shared ovens or arranged a baking day when lots of treats like cakes, biscuits or bread were baked.

Nan taught me how to make cakes. I can remember her clearly telling me that an 8-ounce cake would need 8 ounces each of butter, sugar and flour and 4 eggs; a 6-once cake would need 6 ounces of everything and 3 eggs; a 4-ounce cake would require … I'm sure you can see the pattern forming. It's all Nan's fault that I never need to look at a cake recipe. The measurements are in my head. On the one hand, this is great, but on the other hand, I need to pay attention when creating new cakes and make sure that I write down what I'm doing.

I'm a big fan of a classic Victoria sponge filled with blackcurrant jam, but here's something a little more fancy. Be careful with the amount of rose water you use as it can completely overpower the bake.

SERVES 8

215g caster sugar
215g unsalted butter, softened
4 eggs
215g self-raising flour
50g ground pistachios

prep: 30 minutes, cook: 30 minutes

Preheat the oven to 160°C fan/180°C/gas mark 4. Grease and line the bottom and sides of two 20cm/8-inch cake tins.

Cream the sugar and butter with a hand whisk until light and add the eggs one at a time, adding a little flour with the final egg to stop the mixture from splitting. Add the flour and mix with a spatula until all the ingredients are combined.

Divide the mixture between the two tins and smooth the batter with the spatula, leaving a little in the bowl to taste!

Bake in the oven for 20-25 minutes, or until an inserted skewer comes out clean. Leave to cool in the tins for a round 15 minutes before removing and leaving to cool completely on a wire rack.

While the cakes are baking and cooling, make a simple pistachio brittle to decorate the cake. Place the 100g caster sugar into a small saucepan and warm over a medium heat. The sugar will start to dissolve around the edges and start to turn golden. Swirl the pan gently to disperse the heat until all the sugar has dissolved then add the ground pistachios. Stir briefly then pour out onto a tray lined with greaseproof paper, being careful as it will be very hot. Leave to cool completely and harden.

Once the brittle and the cakes have cooled, whip the cream with the tablespoon of caster sugar and the rose water until it just holds its

FILLING

300ml double cream

½ tsp rose water

1 tbsp caster sugar to sweeten

150g raspberry jam (homemade page 62)

about 125g fresh raspberries

100g caster sugar, plus extra to dust

75g pistachios, shelled

shape – it should be soft and cloud-like, not stiff and bordering on splitting.

Place one of the cakes onto a pretty plate or cake stand and spread the jam on top, leaving a border the width of a raspberry all the way around the edge. Place the fresh raspberries equally around the edge leaving a gap of about a raspberry width again between each one.

Spoon ⅓ of the cream into a piping bag fitted with a plain or star nozzle and pipe neatly between the raspberries, spreading the remaining cream in the middle. Break up the brittle by either popping it into a food processor or bashing it with a rolling pin – it all depends on your mood! Sprinkle some of the smaller pieces of brittle on the cream filling before sandwiching the other cake on top, pressing down lightly so as not to squeeze cream and raspberries out of the sides. There should be enough cream left in the piping bag to pipe a couple of neat rounds on top of the cake. Finish by decorating with some more fresh raspberries and the blitzed/bashed up pistachio brittle.

NAN'S TRADITIONAL WELSH CAKES

These cakes are quintessentially Welsh. They're delicious little teatime treats that are traditionally made for St David's Day. To me, they exude home comfort which is why I usually make a batch and post them to my husband wherever he may be in the world.

Here's Nan's traditional recipe with half lard and half fat. Now, I know that some aren't big fans of lard, but I'd rather you reduce the quantity than remove it altogether. The lard keeps the Welsh cakes moist and also gives a beautifully flaky texture to the crumb. During wartime Britain, butter was in short supply, and so the home baker adapted their trusty recipes and used lard instead.

In many farmhouses across Wales, including my own family's farm, Welsh cakes were served at teatime with hot tea, jam and possibly a little cheese if there was any left. They're the perfect teatime partner of bara brith (recipe on page 30). I can also guarantee that they travel very well should you want to send a care package with some homemade treats to a loved one far away.

MAKES 30

450g self-raising flour

100g lard, cold and cubed (vegetable lard/fat works well)

100g butter, cold and cubed

225g caster sugar

125g currants

2 eggs (beaten with a little milk)

1 tablespoon of golden syrup

¾ tsp of ground nutmeg

¾ tsp of cinnamon

prep: 25 minutes, cook: 25 minutes

Place a bakestone or heavy frying pan over a low heat to warm up. Place the flour and spices into a large bowl, then rub in the lard and butter until the mixture resembles breadcrumbs. Mix in the sugar and currants and then add the beaten eggs and golden syrup. Try slightly heating the syrup so that it's easier to mix with the other ingredients.

Bring the ingredients together in the bowl until it forms a ball of dough, but don't over work the mixture. Tip the dough out onto a lightly floured surface and roll to a thickness of 1cm. I tend to divide the dough in half or into thirds to do this as I find it easier to handle, plus it's not being overworked.

Cut out into 5cm rounds, grease the bakestone/frying pan with a little lard or butter and cook the Welsh cakes until they are a nut-brown. Remember to grease the pan in between each batch and don't over-crowd the pan. They should take between 2-3 minutes each side.

Once baked, sprinkle liberally with caster sugar. They're absolutely delicious eaten hot from the bakestone. If any survive for long enough to cool down, store in an air-tight container, in a cool place and eat within 3-5 days.

BUFFALO CHICKEN DIP

I'm sure you've gathered that I'm a big fan of using leftovers and having minimal food waste. I'm also a very sociable person and love having people over for gatherings – which always revolve around food of course. This recipe is something that I tasted while on one of my trips across the pond to see my American family, and although the version I tried was shop-bought, I managed to get the recipe and have tweaked it a little to give it my own personal touch.

This is one of those dips that won't be around for long – it's very moreish! Serve with some plain crisps or tortilla chips and enjoy with plenty of friends. It's a perfect accompaniment to any sporting event, especially a Welsh rugby international or when the Superbowl is on, which is quite often judging by the amount of times my husband requests this dip.

SERVES 4-6

leftover chicken legs, thighs and wings from the roast chicken recipe (page 162)

225g soft/cream cheese

125g hot sauce/Buffalo sauce

125g ranch dressing

4 spring onions, chopped

1 green pepper, chopped

1 fresh green chilli or 2-3 tbsp of jarred jalapeño peppers, chopped

100g Red Leicester cheese, grated

prep: 15 minutes, cook: 20 minutes

Preheat the oven to 160°C fan/180°C/gas mark 4 and strip the meat from the legs, thighs and wings and shred/chop a little into bite-sized pieces. Place the meat directly into a medium oven dish along with all the other ingredients and stir well to combine. Taste to check the balance, adding more Buffalo sauce if you fancy it a bit hotter.

Bake in the oven for about 15-20 minutes to warm through and melt the cheese. Serve hot with crisps and beer.

DADDY EGGS & SOLDIERS

My husband and my mother are both fans of boiled eggs and it's their go-to solo supper when I or my dad are away. Mam always goes on about how amazing eggs are, claiming they're the best fast food in the world.

When Matt has boiled eggs and soldiers for breakfast he will often have to make extra as Alys will usually eat half of his after finishing her own. They're therefore not called boiled eggs in our house; they're called Daddy Eggs, in honour of Matt, and are frequently requested when the girls are missing him when he's away.

Traditionally served with toast cut into fingers or soldiers, here I make some tasty baked asparagus and pancetta soldiers for added flavour. The girls approve.

SERVES 2

4 eggs (2 per person)
a splash of vinegar
10-12 asparagus spears
10-12 pancetta rashers
a little olive oil
pepper
25g Parmesan cheese, grated

prep: 10 minutes, cook: 10 minutes

Preheat the grill to medium-high and line a baking tray with some foil. Boil a kettle for the eggs and add a splash of vinegar to a medium saucepan, adding the boiled water when ready.

Wrap the asparagus spears with a rasher of pancetta and place onto the prepared baking tray with a drizzle of olive oil and some cracked black pepper. Place under the grill, turning every minute or so until the pancetta is crispy.

Meanwhile, carefully add the eggs to the hot water, and bring back up to the boil. For a soft egg, cook for about 5 minutes.

Once the eggs are ready serve them with the asparagus soldiers with grated Parmesan cheese. A couple of traditionally toasted bread soldiers are also permitted to accompany the Daddy Eggs. Enjoy with a brew.

CHEAT'S BUTTER CHICKEN CURRY

We are a family of curry lovers and I could quite happily eat it every day. It's frequently requested by my two daughters and my husband is very good at making it if he has a recipe to follow. I grew up eating curries thanks to my parents. When she was growing up Mam's best friend was Indian and Mam would regularly go over to her house where she would be greeted with a feast of different dishes made by her mum.

I have fond memories of Mam and Dad making tandoori chicken for supper when we were young; marinating chicken in yoghurt and spices and then roasting it in the oven with cauliflower, serving it with rice, raita, a salad and a chopped-up banana. It wasn't spicy hot, but full of flavour and vibrant colours. With so much going on – I loved it.

When I weaned my daughters onto solid food I wanted to make sure that it was full of flavour, so chicken curry became a firm favourite with them both from a young age and is still a midweek highlight of the meal planning in our house.

Curries can take a while to make, but there are some great recipes available that don't take hours to prepare. When it comes to feeding two young children during the week, speed is of the essence when trying to get them to after-school activities with something nutritious and tasty in their stomachs.

Nan has recently started eating and enjoying curry for the first time too – in her mid-90s. It has taken me years to get her to try a mild curry, with me promising her that it will be tasty and not too hot. She made her own lamb curry and loved it. I guess the saying that you can't teach an old dog new tricks, doesn't apply to an adventurous nan in her mid-90s.

Here's a recipe inspired by my ultimate food hero Rick Stein. I love his recipe for butter chicken, and one day, the girls asked for it but I didn't have 5½ hours to follow every step, and so my own cheat's version was created and is now used as an emergency when the girls need their curry fix.

I tend to use leftover chicken, which speeds things up, or just add vegetables and chickpeas instead. The sauce is just delicious and can be used for meat or veg.

SERVES 4

leftover chicken (no need to marinade) or 6 chicken thighs

MARINADE

80g plain yoghurt – Greek or natural

2 garlic cloves, grated

2cm fresh ginger, grated

½ tsp each of turmeric, cumin, coriander and garam masala

a good pinch of salt

prep: 20 minutes, cook: 30 minutes

If using fresh chicken thighs, roughly chop them into bite-sized pieces and place into a medium bowl along with all the marinade ingredients. Stir to combine and coat the chicken, then cover with cling film and pop into the fridge for at least an hour or longer if you have time. If using leftover chicken or vegetables, there's no need for this step – and the curry will still taste delicious.

The sauce can be made ahead and reheated when ready to serve. Place the oil in a pan over a low-medium heat and add the grated garlic and ginger then fry gently for a couple of minutes. Add the spices and cook for a minute before adding the passata, boiling water and creamed coconut. Simmer for about 10 minutes over a low heat then add the ground almonds. Taste and season with salt.

PS: I don't actually use any butter in the recipe.

For the sauce

1 tbsp vegetable oil

7 garlic cloves, grated

7cm fresh ginger (I keep mine in the freezer as it keeps better and is easier to grate)

a good pinch of chilli flakes (add more if you like it hotter)

¾ tsp each of ground cumin, coriander, cinnamon, garam masala and fenugreek seeds

500g passata

300ml boiling water

⅓ block creamed coconut

50g ground almonds

salt to taste – about 1 tsp

TO SERVE

a small bunch of fresh coriander, roughly chopped

a handful of flaked almonds, lightly toasted

enough boiled rice to feed your troop

some chopped tomato, cucumber and red onion mixed with a little salt and lemon juice

If you're using leftover cooked chicken you can chop it up now and add it to heat through in the sauce. If you're using vegetables, chop them to bite-sized pieces – I tend to use broccoli, green beans, peas or carrots – and cook them in the sauce.

If you're using fresh chicken, after it's had at least an hour in the marinade, preheat the oven to 220°C fan/240°C/gas mark 9 and line a tray with foil. Scatter the chicken piece on the foil and cook in the oven for about 12 minutes. Remove the chicken from the oven and add to the sauce and continue to cook over a low heat for about 5 minutes.

Scatter some coriander and flaked almonds on top and serve the curry with some boiled rice and a simple tomato salad.

MAM'S GINGER & ORANGE TRIFLE

I have memories of eating trifle as a child with fluorescent red jelly, custard that could be sliced and cocktail cherries with hundreds and thousands on top. Since then, trifle flavours have become a little more creative with some welcome texture and liqueur surprises as you dive deeper into the bowl to get a spoonful of every layer. They're still popular around Christmas and are considered a dessert worthy of a celebration.

Trifle is a very popular dessert on many Christmas dinner menus across all the forces too, especially the RAF. It's considered a light dessert option alongside Christmas pudding and is traditionally made with finger sponges soaked in sherry, with fruit suspended in jelly, topped with custard and finished with whipped cream.

This recipe is my mother's very exceptional trifle which is reserved for special occasions and welcome-home meals – especially for my husband who begrudgingly shares the dessert with the rest of us. There are a few steps involved in making this dish, but you can prepare a lot in advance, and if it's for a special occasion then I'm sure it's worth that effort.

SERVES 8-10

GINGER CAKE

115g unsalted butter, soft

115g brown sugar

115g self-raising flour

2 eggs

1 tablespoon treacle

1 tbsp ground ginger

1 tsp mixed spice

3 balls stem ginger, finely chopped

GINGER SPICE BISCUITS

25g butter

50g golden caster sugar

50g squeezy honey

115g plain flour

pinch of baking powder

pinch of bicarbonate of soda

¾ teaspoon ground ginger

¼ teaspoon mixed spice

CANDIED ORANGE PEEL

peel of 1 large orange

75g caster sugar

prep: 40 minutes, cook: 30 minutes

Make the cake by firstly creaming the butter, sugar and treacle. Gradually add the eggs and flour with the spices and stem ginger until combined and pour into the tin. Bake for 30 minutes, making sure that a cocktail stick comes out clean when inserted into the middle. Cool in the tin for 10 minutes before removing and cooling on a wire rack.

To make the ginger-spiced biscuits heat the butter, sugar and honey in a small saucepan until melted. Remove from the heat and stir in the flour, spices and baking powder/soda, until the dough forms a ball. Knead on a lightly floured work surface until smooth, wrap in cling film and chill while the cake is baking. The biscuits can be baked at the same oven temperature as the cake. Once the cake is baked and out of the oven, remove the biscuit dough from the fridge and roll out to 5mm thickness. Cut out 15-20 little rounds of dough and place on a baking tray. Bake for 8-10 minutes. Cool on a wire rack.

For the candied orange peel, carefully remove the peel from an orange, making sure not to include any pith, then cut it into strips measuring 0.5cm by 4cm, place in a small saucepan and cover with water. Bring to the boil for 10-15 seconds before straining through a sieve. Return the peel to the same saucepan and add 75ml of water and 75g caster sugar. Bring to the boil then simmer for 3-5 minutes until the liquid is syrupy. Remove the peel and dust in some more caster sugar then leave to cool and dry for at least 30 minutes on a wire rack.

Once the cake has cooled, make the jelly by heating 350ml of orange juice in a saucepan, bringing it to the boil. Soften 4 gelatine leaves in some cold water before adding them to the orange juice away from

ORANGE JELLY

350ml freshly squeezed
orange juice from about 3
large oranges

4 leaves gelatine

CRÈME PÂTISSIÈRE

500ml full fat milk or gold top

125g caster sugar

6 egg yolks

20g plain flour

20g cornflour

CHANTILLY CREAM

250ml double cream

1 tbsp icing sugar to sweeten

ADDITIONAL INGREDIENTS

5 large sweet oranges

orange liqueur – Cointreau or
Grand Marnier

the heat and stir until dissolved. Allow to cool slightly. While the orange juice is cooling, segment 3-5 oranges depending on their size. Cut a very thin layer off the top of the sponge and discard (or eat) and place the remainder on the bottom of the trifle dish. Liberally drizzle some orange liqueur or orange juice over the sponge before adding a layer of orange segments, then pour on the orange jelly and place in the fridge to set for at least 2 hours.

Make the crème pâtissière by heating up the milk with the vanilla pod until boiling. Meanwhile whisk together the eggs, sugar and flour until pale and light. Add the hot milk and combine before putting the mixture back into the saucepan and back on the heat. Stir with a whisk until boiling, let it bubble for a little bit before removing from the heat and pouring it into a clean bowl to cool. Cover with a little cling film directly on top of the crème pâtissière to prevent a skin forming and leave to cool completely before pouring on top of the jelly and sponge layers once they've set.

To make the Chantilly cream whisk the double cream with the icing sugar to medium-stiff peaks, tthen spread evenly over the top of the trifle, creating peaks with the back of a spoon.

If it isn't going to be served straight away, place the trifle in the fridge to firm up before decorating with the spiced ginger biscuits and orange candied peel. Add a touch of edible glitter if you're feeling festive.

CHAPTER 8

IN MEMORIAM

I feel lucky to be part of the military community. It's a world I never thought I'd enter, but it found me and continues to send me on a rollercoaster of emotions and memories. The friendships formed are lifelong and you may only spend a short amount of time with each other depending on the length of the posting, but when you meet up again years later, you just pick up where you left off.

As a military wife, I've lived away from my family and have been left on my own when my husband has been away. The support given to me then was invaluable. I may no longer live near some of my military wife best friends, and can't pop over for coffee or a glass of gin, but knowing that they are only a text message or a phone call away is more than enough. Often, all I need is for one of them to listen, because they understand what I'm going through.

Because of the temporary nature of military postings, new friendships are made quickly – hard and fast – because you're ever aware that the time will always come to move on to the next posting. And when that time comes, leaving friends is hard, especially when you have to do it all the time, so no one ever really says goodbye.

My husband's friendship and support network operates differently. This is due to the nature of the work in the forces. Friendships are made quickly and are strong, meaning that when a loss happens it really hits home.

I felt strongly that I should end the book with something to remember those who we've lost along the way and to honour them and the friendships that keep us going. Be it military or civilian, having your own community there to support you through the tough days and share the good times is what gets us through life.

So thank you to my family and friends, to my community, because I love you all.

LEMON, RASPBERRY & POPPY CELEBRATION CAKE

I wanted to create a simple celebration cake that would suit any occasion. I knew that I wanted it to be decorated with buttercream and finished with edible flowers so that even if you're a beginner at cake decorating, this shouldn't be too difficult yet will look impressive. I wanted the fresh taste of lemon and raspberry to complement the sweet and silky buttercream and for it not to be too heavy to eat. Blueberries make a lovely change if you don't fancy raspberries, but I just love the ruby red colour and tartness that raspberries bring to the finished cake, which matches the lemon perfectly.

SERVES 20

330g caster sugar

330g soft, unsalted butter

6 large eggs

350g self-raising flour

35g ground almonds

zest of 3 lemons

juice of 1 lemon

3 tbsp poppy seeds

150g fresh raspberries

Lemon Swiss Meringue
    Buttercream

4 large egg whites

200g golden caster sugar

400g unsalted butter, soft and
    cut into chunks

zest of 2 lemons

juice of ½ lemon

150g raspberry jam (see recipe
    page xxx)

TO DECORATE

edible flowers

prep: 1½ hours, cook: 30 minutes

Grease and line two 20cm/8-inch cake tins and one deep 15cm/6-inch cake tin. Preheat the oven to 160°C fan/180°C/gas mark 4.

Using an electric whisk, cream together the butter and sugar until light and creamy. Add the eggs 2 at a time, and a little flour towards the end to prevent the mixture from splitting. Add the remaining flour and ground almonds and mix to combine. Add the zest, juice and poppy seeds and stir until all evenly distributed. Divide the mixture between the 3 tins and roughly smooth the tops. Add a handful of fresh raspberries to each tin, scatter evenly on top and then bake in the oven for 25 minutes. The two 8-inch tins will be ready after this time, but the 6-inch cake may need an extra 5 minutes. Insert a skewer to check. If it's cooked, the skewer should come out clean. Leave to cool completely before decorating.

For the Swiss meringue buttercream, place the egg whites and the sugar into the bowl of a freestanding mixer and place over a saucepan of simmering water. Using a balloon whisk, stir the mixture until the sugar has dissolved. Rub a little between your fingers to check. Return the bowl to the mixer and whisk the whites until stiff and glossy and until the bowl has cooled.

Turn the speed down low then slowly add the softened butter a piece at a time, leaving a couple of seconds between each piece so that it can be incorporated into the meringue. Once all the butter has been added, turn the speed back up to medium-high until you have a smooth and thick consistency. Add the lemon zest and juice and mix on low to combine. Use while soft or keep covered for a couple of hours until needed.

To assemble, level the 8-inch cakes and place one onto a serving plate. Spread some of the buttercream over the top along with some of the jam before putting the other 8-inch cake on top. Cover with a thin layer of buttercream, you don't want a thick layer, but don't be mean either. Next, cut the 6-inch cake in half horizontally and level

It's a cake that will truly stand out at any party or gathering.

the top if it has domed slightly while cooking. Place one half on top of the 8-inch cake, cover it with buttercream and jam as you did with the first cake then place the other half on top and cover with buttercream again.

You should now have a 2-tiered cake, filled with jam and buttercream, as well as being covered in buttercream. Decorate with some beautiful, edible flowers. This is a simple and elegant celebration cake with fresh flavours that would suit any occasion.

ACKNOWLEDGMENTS

A big thank you to everyone who made this book possible, especially Marc my editor, Sue at Gomer, Rebecca for her design and Aled for his beautiful photographs – a fantastic team that guided me through the process from concept to print. Diolch yn fawr!

I'd also like to thank the Imperial War Museum for the valuable inspiration I found there, reading through some of its vast food history resources. I've happily spent several hours on my own, wandering its many rooms and sitting quietly reading through boxes of menus, recipes, Ministry of Food leaflets and many other items from the collection. I very much look forward to visiting the museum again soon when I'm next in London.

A thank you goes out to the military community which has shown support to me from all corners of the world! Thank you to all who messaged stories and recipes – it was wonderful to hear about your experiences and memories and I hope that this book will ring true with many of you.

Thank you to my military best friend Vicki and her mum Debs for sharing their story and Margaret's recipe from their time in Hong Kong and also to Kim for her family favourite cheesy hammy eggy dish. Thank you to another military wife friend Eloise who was able to put me in contact with Jane to hear all about the infamous Officers' Wives' Dip – I can confirm that it is delicious!

Thank you to Mam-gu and Aunty 'Rene for inspiring me and never ever telling me to go away when I stood next to them in the kitchen. They were two phenomenal women who I miss dearly but who, I know, are checking in on me from time to time when I'm busy in my own kitchen.

Thank you Nan for being more than just a grandmother – you're more like a big sister who has looked after me and inspired me – and continue to do so. I love you very much Nan!

Thank you just doesn't seem enough to express my gratitude to you Mam and Dad – *Dwi'n caru chi shwd gymaint; diolch am bopeth.*

And finally to Matt, the soldier in my life who inspired this book in the first place; thank you for letting me share all the ups and downs of military life with you, I wouldn't have it any other way. And to my two little shadows Mari and Alys – *caru chi!*

CONVERSION TABLES

METRIC – IMPERIAL WEIGHTS CONVERSIONS

Metric	Imperial
30g	1oz
55g	2oz
110g	4oz (1/4 lb)
170g	6oz
225g	8oz (1/2 lb)
285g	10oz
340g	12oz (3/4 lb)
400g	14oz
450g	16oz (1 lb)

OVEN TEMPERATURES

°C - fan	°C	°F	Gas mark
50	70	150	¼
60	80	175	¼
80	100	200	½
90	110	225	½
110	130	250	1
120	140	275	1
130	150	300	2
150	170	325	3
160	180	350	4
170	190	375	5
180	200	400	6
200	220	425	7
210	230	450	8

METRIC – IMPERIAL LENGTHS CONVERSIONS

Metric	Imperial
1cm	½ inch
2.5cm	1 inch
5cm	2 inches
10cm	4 inches
15cm	6 inches
20cm	8 inches
25cm	10 inches
30cm	12 inches

INDEX